Enjoy!

Ernie

Ernie Wendell

GRAND-Stories

101+ Bridges of love joining
grandparents and grandkids

Compiled and Edited by
Ernie Wendell

Illustrated by
Timothy E. Wiegenstein

Friendly Oaks Publications
Pleasanton, TX   78064

Published by:
  Friendly Oaks Publications
  P.O. Box 662
  Pleasanton, TX 78064-0662 (USA)
  (830) 569-3586
  fax: (830) 281-2617

Last digit is print number: 6 5 4 3 2 1

Library of Congress Cataloging-in-Publication Data

GRAND-stories : 101+ bridges of love joining grandparents and grandkids / compiled and edited by Ernie Wendell ; illustrated by Timothy E. Wiegenstein.
  p. cm.
  ISBN 1-878878-58-1 (hardcover)
  1. Grandparent and child--Anecdotes. I. Wendell, Ernie, 1930-

HQ759.9 .G69 2000
306.874'5--dc21   99-059444

$21.95 Hardcover

Dedication

It seems my children grew up when I wasn't looking. I was busy. Quite suddenly they were not children anymore. To show me all that I had missed, they presented me with grandchildren. It is to them, my seven wonderful grandkids, that I dedicate this book.

Lauren: Our first grandchild, now a college student. You warm my heart and fill me up with your energy and love. From then, until now, you have been a true joy and blessing.

Meridith: Our second grandchild, a junior in high school. You have been and remain my princess with golden hair and sky-blue eyes. You hug me like you mean it. I find great joy in your presence.

Stephen: Our first grandson. You are a welcome addition, a boy to carry on the family name. You are a sweet spirit who will do us great honor. You have all the tools.

Amanda: Our fourth grandchild. You hold my heart in your hands. We share a love that knows no bounds—as close as father and daughter.

Ariana: Our fifth grandchild. My blond, brown-eyed nymph. You live too far away, but still you eagerly jump into my arms at first sight. You fill me with your love.

JohnLee: Our second grandson, sixth grandchild. You reach for me with uplifted arms, a full smile, and a giving spirit. I find you so easy to love.

Alyssa: Our seventh grandchild. Newly arrived, not yet a week old. I see my dad in your beautiful face. You will be special.

To all of you I give my love forever. Remember me; I'm your grandpa.

A Legacy of Love

I thought I'd leave a legacy, a living part of me.
Something you would recognize, something you could see.

At first I thought to plant a tree, a mighty Oak or two.
Or maybe plant a tree of fruit to someday feed a few.

But, no, that didn't satisfy; it didn't pass the test.
It had to be the perfect choice—the one and only best.

What would it be, this legacy, this legacy of love?
I needed help to fix the choice. I prayed to God above.

God answered me without a pause; He whispered in my ear.
I heard His voice on wings of prayer. He made it all so clear.

"Your grandchildren are your legacy; they'll never let you die.
Your memory will live with them; they'll always hold it high.

Your bond is love, and love unfolds a legacy so pure,
With love like that there is no fear—your legacy's secure."

— Ernie Wendell
Copyright ©1999

Table of Contents

Foreword
Preface
Acknowledgments

Part One: *A Smile or Two*

Part Two: *Faith and Courage*

Part Three: *Life's Moments*

Part Four: *Portraits*

Afterword

Foreword

Look at the numbers. Today's 60,000,000 grandparents in the United States are expected to grow to 96,000,000 million in the next decade. This will happen as Baby Boomers become grandparents. At that time, one in every two persons over the age of 35 will be a grandparent. Unlike the stereotype, grandparents are very active people, many of whom are in mid-career. And they are young! AARP tells us that the median age for first-time grandparents is just 46. And, according to the U.S. Census Bureau, almost 4,000,000 grandparents are raising and providing full-time support for their grandchildren.

Grandparents bring families together in one of life's great second chances. They connect generations, and their influence on society is second to none. The grandparent-grandchild connection is powerful, and, I believe, spiritually-based.

For all these reasons, this country's best days are ahead.

I also know about grandparents through my work as the manufacturer of Alexis™ brand clothing for newborns. Grandparents are our primary customers. In addition, we sponsor the Warren Featherbone Foundation, whose principle mission is to raise awareness of the importance of interdependent relationships in society.

But that doesn't explain all of the grandparenting phenomenon. The author of this book, Ernie Wendell, knows exactly how to convey the hopes, joys, and challenges of being a grandparent— *GRAND-Stories*.

Thank you, Ernie, for your great sensitivity in bringing together this collection. The message is timely—the truths timeless.

—Charles E. "Gus" Whalen, Jr.
President and CEO, The Warren Featherbone Company
Author, *The Featherbone Principle: A Declaration of of Interdependence*

Preface

Enter the grandparent. Loving, considerate, patient, kind, and very willing to make time, special time, for grandchildren. How wonderful. It is who I want to be.

Last year, October 1998, I was asked to participate in Grandparents' Day at Cresset Christian Academy in Durham, North Carolina. My granddaughter, Amanda, attends that school and was then in the second grade. I was to be part of the program for two reasons: First, I am a grandfather. Second, I speak professionally.

With some hesitation I agreed to share in this celebration to honor grandparents. I hesitated because of a very busy schedule; I accepted because of Amanda's teacher, Mrs. Eldersveld. I found it impossible to say "no" to her; she was that charming. And, of course, it was an opportunity to make Amanda proud of her granddad.

I want her to be proud of me.

The audience, grandparents and grandchildren alike, was spontaneous, responsive, excited, and just pleased with the opportunity to be together. They enjoyed the program. I was reminded of that popular bumper sticker: "If I had known grandchildren were so much fun, I would have had them *first*."

Hey, if I had know that grandparents were such a marvelous audience, I would have found them sooner!

Being a grandparent has been and remains a positive experience for me, one of the true joys of my life. I want it to be the same for all grandparents. As I accepted the opportunity to share in the program at Amanda's school—an idea was born. The idea came as a direct result of that receptive audience so tuned in to the stories of grandparent-grandkid relationships. I wanted to stoke the fires of this very special and ongoing love affair. I wanted to add some new life to an association as old as time itself.

How would I do it? What method would I use? How could I reach that vast assembly of the world's grandparents and grandkids? I would first collect their stories. I began the process by collecting, first-hand, true-to-life stories about grandparents loving grandkids (and vice-versa). I went out to the universe and asked for their stories, and the universe responded with dozens of personal anecdotes that pierced my heart and tickled my funnybone. I then needed only to place the material in book form for others to savor.

A book to compile, a new audience to reach—a career change in the making. I was ready.

What a remarkable journey it has been. I especially welcomed the splendid opportunity to interact with some truly wonderful and loving people. Many of them, but certainly not all of them, are fellow members of the National Speakers Association (NSA), who were most willing, even eager, to share their personal stories. They were a pure joy to work with as we endeavored to massage and smooth their intimate descriptions of important events and people in their lives. In addition, the contributors were so encouraging to me as the work continued—an experience I will long remember.

The quality of the *GRAND-Stories* offered has been amazing. Depending on the focus of the narrative, these stories have drawn from me both the tears of sadness and the joys of laughter. They will do the same for you. These wonderful *GRAND-Stories* will be read and enjoyed alike by the many generations that compose the modern family. In the reading, and in the sharing, may we move closer together and connect the generations.

In the gathering of the stories, it became apparent that, for many different reasons, grandparents are often very special in the lives of their grandkids. In many instances, grandparents have found it necessary to once again assume the role of parent and raise their grandkids. Some grandparents have taken on the responsibility out of pure love and with a genuine concern for the well-being of their grandkids. Others, who would have preferred to remain in the role of grandparent, who were resting from the toils of an earlier life, have had to take on the parental responsibility because there was no one else to do it. Often there are financial problems and legal tangles to overcome; a challenge of our time. The challenge is being met, and generations to come will be the better for it.

The *GRAND-Stories* tell of a marvelous love affair that exists between the generations. They tell of a sharing and an intimacy that is found in no other relationship under God's sun (unless it is the parent-child relationship); a loving, caring, nurturing kinship that dates back to the beginning of time.

Grandparents, read these stories to your grandkids. Grandchildren, read these stories to your grandparents. In the process, love each other with all your might. As a result, the world will be a better place in which to live.

—EJW

Acknowledgments

To all those who responded to my call for stories I am deeply grateful. This treasury of *GRAND-Stories* was compiled as a labor of love. It could not have happened without the support of the story contributors. The journey from first idea to final realization was shared with so many.

The contributing authors were a joy to work with during the editing process. Egos were set aside as every effort was made to flow each story to the reader in a smooth and clear manner. In this book the reader is king or queen and the writer the servant.

My thanks to each writer who stayed the course until we finally arrived at this successful conclusion. I am indebted to you beyond measure for your support. You have been an inspiration.

Working with Jim Sutton, the publisher, has been a revelation as to how two people can work together smoothly and in concert. Jim's goal, from the outset, was to produce an end product that was truly worthy of the efforts of all the contributors. I owe him my sincere thanks. In pursuit of his goal, Jim put together a quality team. My thanks to Robert Howard for a cover design that is an absolute delight to behold. Tim Wiegenstein's illustrations of the stories brought yet another dimension to the whole project. Indeed, the talents of Robert and Tim changed the book from a collection of stories to a work of art. And finally, thanks go to Dawn Lee Wakefield for her diligent job of copyediting this book.

—EJW

Part One

A Smile or Two

T hese stories fill our need to laugh and connect with our more spontaneous nature. There's no one better than a child to teach us how.

1

Ask, and You Will Hear
by Geraldine Markel

Charlie is our 18-month-old grandson. He's learning all the sounds that the animals make; we are helping.

"Charlie, what does a cow say?" we ask.

"Moo," he answers.

"Charlie, what does a horse say?"

"Neigh, neigh."

Then, to satisfy our grandparent curiosity, we introduced a very special question: "Charlie, what does your mommy say?"

Charlie hesitates for just a few seconds, then shouts, "Mommy say NO! NO! NO!"

Geraldine (Geri) Markel is a lucky grandmother. Her six grandchildren live in Ann Arbor, Michigan, and there are many wonderful opportunities for fun and laughter.

2

How Old?
by Lois Wyse

Samuel, age 6, was sitting next to Grandmother at services in the temple.

"The Lord our God, the Lord is ONE," the rabbi intoned.

"Grandma," whispered Samuel, "When will He be TWO?"

Reprinted from the book, *You Wouldn't Believe What My Grandchild Did* by Lois Wyse (Simon and Schuster, 1995). This story is used with the kind permission of the author and publisher.

3

A Penny Saved

by Bruce Wilkinson

Some years ago my cousin Becky, who was then 7 years old, accompanied my Aunt Betty (her grandmother) on a train trip to California. At that time the ticket fare would be reduced by half if a passenger was under the age of 7. Not one to waste money, Aunt Betty advised her granddaughter that, should anyone ask during this trip, she was <u>6</u> years old.

As chance would have it, two nuns came into the coach car and sat down near them. After a few minutes, one of the nuns smiled at Becky and remarked, "You're a cute little girl. How old are you?"

With only a moment's hesitation, Becky responded, "I'm 6." And then she quickly added, "My grandmother can't afford for me to be 7 anymore."

Bruce Wilkinson, Certified Speaking Professional, is a motivational humorist and corporate trainer from Gretna, Louisiana.

4

My Best Introduction

by Art Linkletter

A few years ago my 9-year-old grandchild Stacey asked me if I'd come out to her school and talk to her class. Naturally, being a granddad, I said, "Yes." As you know, *that's* what grandfathers are for.

In return for getting me to make this free public appearance, the teacher assigned Stacey to make my introduction.

A few days later the young lady was back visiting with me, inquiring what she could say to give an introduction. I replied: "Darling, I have interviewed over 20,000 children on my TV show, and I never told one of them what to say or how to say it. They all lived through it and gave us something entirely new and interesting to think about. I am sure you will think of something appropriate and timely to say; I'll leave it up to you."

When the big day arrived, the nervous young lady took me by the hand, led me out before a crowd of fellow classmates, and gave this introduction:

"This is my grandfather. He's 70 years old. And he's *still* alive!"

(Stacey and I were laughing about this story last week while reminiscing about her growing-up years. Our talk concluded with, "Grandpa, I have one more introduction to make in about 8 months that I think will please you. I will be handing into your arms your 12th great-grandchild.)

Art Linkletter is still alive at 87, and going strong. He's on CBS Friday nights at 8:00 p.m. with Bill Cosby and *Kids Say the Darndest Things!*

5

Our Special Day
by Doc Blakely

When my granddaughter Torie was about 5 years old, I started taking her to the Houston Livestock Show and Rodeo. It was our "special day out." It was a one-day, annual event that was important to both of us. No one else was allowed to go.

We had a regular routine we had worked out over the years. First, we took in all the livestock exhibits. Then we attended the matinee rodeo. After the rodeo we would spend the rest of the afternoon at the carnival. We would then return to the rodeo for the evening performance. We topped off the evening by returning to the carnival so we could take in all the rides.

We always stayed until they closed the place.

One particular year stands out as being very special; Torie was about 9 at the time. We were on our way back to the car, walking hand-in-hand and eating cotton candy at midnight. It had been a good time of sharing. We had held onto each other tightly and screamed together as we rode the wild rides.

We were acting as silly as only a pair like us is allowed to behave. In the midst of our shared joy, she looked up at me and said, "PaPa, I sure am glad you're *my* grandfather. I've had a wonderful time."

I smiled down at my granddaughter and said, "Well, Torie, I'm glad you're *my* granddaughter. I've had a pretty ridiculous time myself."

She then wistfully added: "Of course I know I'll grow older and grow up. You'll grow older too, PaPa—but you'll *never* grow up!"

Doc Blakely is a popular speaker and humorist from Wharton, Texas.

6

A Granny by any Other Name

by Hope Mihalap

"Aren't you excited about your first grandchild?"

"Uh ... yeah," I said nervously.

"You don't sound very excited."

"Well," I explained, "I'm worried about the Yaya."

"The what?"

"You see, if you're of Greek descent, you know all Greek grandmothers are called 'Yaya,' and all Greek grandfathers are 'Papou' (stress the second syllable)."

Now, did I really want the kid to call me Yaya? After all, look what that word conjured up to me: an elderly lady with white hair, sometimes overweight, wearing a black dress and ground grippers. I don't look like that (yet). And I don't *want* to look like that.

So I considered the English alternatives. Granny? Worse; rimless glasses and maybe no teeth were added to the image. Grandma? A pretty close second to Granny. Grandmother? Too formal (and kind of snooty-sounding, too).

My Russian-born husband suggested his language. "For you, Babushka; for me, Dyedushka."

"That's all very well," I thought. Babies don't fear foreign words, so they wouldn't have any problems with the names. But, you know, Babushka *also* infers a little old lady with a black headscarf and no teeth.

Right back to the Granny Syndrome.

I can't begin to tell you how much all this concerned me. Alex, our little granddaughter, came along, and whenever I baby-sat her, I would make small suggestions to her. I would say things like, "Come to Grandmama!" I had already decided that anything even close to my favorite mother word, Mama, would be acceptable to me.

As she began to talk a little, our granddaughter didn't really call me much of anything. Then her daddy, our son, solved the dilemma for me. I hadn't seen Alex for several weeks, and when she came into the room she toddled right over to me and called out, "Yaya!"

She called out that name in the cutest baby voice I had ever heard. Gone forever were my visions of ancient crones.

How had this happened? Well, my son confessed that he had shown her my photograph and taught her to say the word. All it meant to her (and to him) was me, with no funny-looking job description attached. It was then that I realized that what *I* had pictured as a Yaya was absolutely irrelevant. It was the voice of the one saying the word that made all the difference. It was her baby tones that described the very Yaya I wanted to be.

In fact, she could have used any word she wanted, and I would still have been her slave.

We have a second granddaughter now, living in Germany. I understand that her German grandmother is prompting her to say "Grossmama." As for me, I'll start pushing the "Yaya" when they come to visit. But in all of this I've learned one thing: It's *all* up to the kid.

Hey, you don't think she'll call me Fritz, do you?

Hope Mihalap is an award-winning humorist who lives in Virginia. Her favorite topics are language humor and the true experiences of her multicultural family.

7

Cheers

by Terry Fitzgerald Sieck

I had been working with my 3-year-old grandson, Bijan, on the subject of manners. One day he came dashing into the kitchen yelling, "Coke! Coke! Coke!"

"You may have a Coke," I replied. "But what do you say first?"

"Peeease?" he responded. (Bijan had trouble saying "L"s, but the sincerity was certainly there.)

I poured the drink into a glass and handed it to him. "Now what do you say?" I asked.

A broad smile crossed his lips; his face lit up with the glow of knowing. He raised his glass, and, with great confidence, shouted out, "Cheers!"

While I was the one who had taught him "Cheers," it was not the answer I expected. I laughed, of course, as he dashed out of the kitchen.

Later, while sharing this story with a friend, I reflected how Bijan had become an unexpected answer to a special request of mine. I had been widowed at the age of 44; my husband Ron and I had been without children. In fact, both Ron and I had ourselves been only-children. My parents and Ron's father had passed on, and his mother lived far away. I was left with very little family. My constant prayer was that I might find another good husband and not spend the rest of my life alone.

Three years after Ron's, death I met a wonderful man (a widower), and we were married. The answer to my prayer for a husband, however, came with an unexpected blessing. My new husband came to me with three grown daughters, their husbands, and Bijan. (Since then, there have been three more grandchildren)."

So, as I thought of Bijan saying "Cheers!" instead of "Thank you" for the Coke, I also thought of the "Cheers!" he and the other grandchildren have brought into my life. Somehow, the special gift of my grandchildren deserves more than just a "Thanks"; it merits a really happy exclamation. So, I raise my glass to the One on high with, "Cheers! And thanks for this miraculous gift of a new life."

Terry Fitzgerald Sieck is an author and professional speaker who lives in San Diego, California. Lsieck@pacbell.net

8

Crazy Cows

by Vilis Ozols

Grandma Anna, my wife's Latvian grandmother, lives in the Chicago area near O'Hare airport. This is *not* a rural area; it's right there in the urban "concrete jungle." That's why I was missing the point and having such a difficult time understanding what Grandma Anna was trying to tell me.

Perhaps you've had one of those disjointed conversations where you sort of know the words a person is speaking, but you're not sure what they're trying to say—what they're *really* talking about.

Well, Grandma was getting extremely agitated about some *cows*. Cows in urban Chicago (aside, I suppose, from the one that started the Great Chicago Fire)? With Grandma it was *cows* this, *cows* that, and *cows* do and *cows* don't. I just didn't understand. Grandma was not senile, so I was puzzled. Was this a flashback to the old country? My vision was one of displaced cows eating her flowers and wandering through the neighborhood.

I finally worked up the courage to tell her I didn't have a clue. "It's dose cows *again*!" she exclaimed in exasperation. "Dey ... dey ... dey ..." In her frustration she couldn't get it out.

"What is it, Grandma? What about those cows?"

"Dose ... dose ...*cows*! Dey win dat world championship, and, dis city—it go crazy *again*!"

She was, of course, referring to the great Chicago *Bulls* basketball team. The team's name, however, wasn't quite the same after it was filtered through this ethnic grandparent's perspective.

And now—Michael Jordan, and—da Chicago Cows!"

Vilis Ozols lives in Golden, Colorado with his wife, Andra and his two sons. He is the president and founder of The Ozols Business Group, providing leadership training, motivational speaking, and business consulting. (800) 353-1030. www.ozols.com

2

Hail to the Chief

by Lois Wyse

Annelle was pushing her first grandchild, Maximillian, along Madison Avenue when her husband said, "You just keep walking along, paying no attention to what's going on. Don't you notice all these people turning around to look at you?"

"Of course I see them turning to look," she answered smugly. "But they're not looking at me. They're looking at this beautiful grandchild."

"No, I don't think so," her husband answered. "You see, you are humming, and your humming is so loud ..."

"And what's wrong with that?" the new grandmother asked defiantly.

"Nothing, dear," her husband assured her, "but the tune you are humming is 'Hail to the Chief.'"

Reprinted from the book, *You Wouldn't Believe What My Grandchild Did* by Lois Wyse (Simon and Schuster, 1995). This story is used with the kind permission of the author and publisher.

10

Letter Perfect

by John Daly

This is a story I love to tell my grandchildren, for they enjoy hearing about things that happened to their parents when they were kids. This particular event took place when we had only the first five of our eight tykes.

We were sightseeing around my hometown of Washington, D.C., driving one of a succession of used limousines that served as transportation for our growing family. We arrived at Arlington Cemetery for one of the Veteran's Day ceremonies.

We were walking around the grounds, taking in all the sights and just sensing the beauty of the place when one of the kids asked us about the headstones. You know, the usual who, why, and when. We explained the purpose of headstones as best we could, and that seemed to cover it pretty well.

After a moment or two of reflection LuAnne, our oldest, had another question. "But who writes the words on the markers?" she asked. We explained further that those who are left behind do their best to compose the right words for the headstones.

After a few moments of deep thought, LuAnne solemnly declared, "Well, don't let Deirdre write mine. She makes backwards 'N's."

John Jay Daly is president of Daly Communications. He is a professional speaker, consultant, and the author of two books, *Mastering Meetings* and *The Communicator's Chapbook* (Chester Publications, 1991, 1999). (301) 656-2510. johndaly@erols.com www.speakers.com/jdaly.html

11

Who Won?

by Lois Wyse

Phyllis played hide-and-seek with her grandfather, and—like many small children—she covered her eyes in the belief that, if she did, Grandfather could not see her.

Upstairs and downstairs he would look for Phyllis; under beds and in closets he would call her name. She loved their game. And so did Grandfather. But his favorite of all their hiding and seeking—the time he recounts to his friends—came on the day he went down to the basement to look for Phyllis, then chased back up the steps, only to find her standing at the head of the stairway.

"Was I there?" she chirped.

Reprinted from the book, *You Wouldn't Believe What My Grandchild Did* by Lois Wyse (Simon and Schuster, 1995). Used with the kind permission of the author and publisher.

12

The Strange Menu

by Geraldine Markel

One fine evening my husband and I took our 7-year-old grandson, Dylan, out to dinner. It is always a special treat for us, and we look forward to the time we share with him. On this particular evening we chose a nice Chinese restaurant.

We were seated at a table that was preset with those special paper placemats so popular in Chinese restaurants (those placemats that display all the various animals representing birth years in the Chinese culture).

Dylan began to carefully examine his placemat. He searched the border, rapidly moving his finger across the mat. After a moment he looked up at me with a puzzled expression on his young face.

With real amazement in his disbelieving voice, he called out, "Dog? Horse? Rat? Goat? Snake? What kind of restaurant is this? My mother doesn't let me order *this* kind of stuff."

An honest mistake; he thought he was reading from the menu. We proceeded to order from the *real* menu, and we all enjoyed a lovely meal.

Geraldine (Geri) Markel is a lucky grandmother. Her six grandchildren live in Ann Arbor, Michigan, and there are many opportunities for fun and laughter.

13

Whistle While You Drink

by Bob Perks

Recently, while walking through a store, I heard the most beautiful whistling. I was immediately captured by the pure tones of the trills. It sounded professional; bird sounds of the most wonderful kind.

As I turned into the next aisle, I located the delightful sound. There, right in front of me, a woman was taking product inventory. Computer in hand, she was happily whistling along with the sounds of the season.

"So, this is where 'Whistle While You Work' comes from!" I commented, admiring the beauty of her melodies.

The lady stopped what she was doing and turned her attention to me. "Oh, no," she said. "It's whistle while you *drink*!"

I guess I looked puzzled. She explained with a story.

When she was very young, her grandmother once confided in her that every time Grandpa would go down into the basement (supposedly to check the furnace), he would sneak a drink from a hidden bottle. The lady in the store recalled many instances of hearing Grandma shout out to Grandpa, "Henry, I don't hear you whistling!"

She explained that Grandma figured that, if Grandpa was whistling, he *couldn't* be drinking. That's what she thought—but she was wrong. "You see," she explained, "Grandpa taught me how to drink and whistle at the *same* time. Now, I don't drink, but the whistling still makes me smile."

In my rush to shop, had I not stopped to comment on her rare talent, I would have missed a delightful story. So, whistle while you work. It lets the world know you are a happy person, and it lets your spouse know you're staying out of trouble.

And, in the hustle and bustle of life, stop occasionally and speak to strangers. They might have a wondrous gift to share.

Bob Perks is a professional speaker and the author of *The Flight of a Lifetime!* (Sparrow Distribution, 1997). (570) 696-2581. www.bobperks.com

<u>14</u>

Your Privilege

by Lois Blanton

We are active grandparents who love to spend time with all four of our grandchildren. One evening my husband and I were taking our grandchildren out for a special dinner at a pizza place. They loved this dinner spot because it had a game room for children.

Before we left the house, I overheard my daughter talking to the children (ages 3 through 9). She was telling them emphatically, "You are not to ask for money to play in the game room. Ma-ma and Pa-pa are treating you to supper, and that's enough. *Don't* ask them for any money."

Well, even when kids are trying hard to follow directions they can put their own twist on a situation. When our 6-year-old grandson finished his supper he snuggled up to Pa-pa and commented: "We can't ask you for any money. But if you'd like to give us some—that's your privilege!"

Lois Blanton is a mother and grandmother. She is also the secretary to the Dean of the Divinity School at Duke University in Durham, North Carolina.

15

A Widower in Waiting

by J. B. Morris

When I was a young man, my grandfather came to live with us on an extended visit. He had been a widower for some time. I soon discovered, however, that he had a lively interest in (and an eye for) the ladies, even though he was 86 years old.

Shortly after his arrival, we were sitting out on the front porch engaged in rather routine family conversation when my grandfather suddenly asked me a pointed question: "Son, are there any widows living around here."

"I only know of one who lives nearby, Granddad," I responded.

"Who is she, and where does she live?"

Her name is Linnie Bollie," I replied. I pointed to a house across the road. "Right over there. That's where she lives." Then the conversation changed, and I didn't really think any more about it.

About 3 weeks later, my grandfather approached me to ask if I would drive him over to the preacher's house. My curiosity got the best of me, so I asked him why he wanted to see the preacher.

"Well, I'm going to get married," he announced. "I've got to talk to the preacher."

"Granddad, who are you going to marry?" I asked.

"Why, Linnie Bollie," he responded. "Who do you think?"

Dr. J. B. Morris is a retired chiropractic physician living in Durham, North Carolina.

16

Blue Plate Special

author unknown

Two little boys were visiting their grandfather, and he took them to a restaurant for lunch. They couldn't make up their minds about what they wanted to eat. Finally the grandfather grinned at the server and said, "Just bring 'em bread and water."

One of the youngsters looked up and quavered, "Can I have ketchup on it?"

Taken from the Web site for the *Foundation for Grandparenting*, and used with their kind permission. www.grandparenting.org

17

Water Them—and They Will Grow

by Sylvia B. Bailey

Justin was 2-and-a-half years old. He was staying with his Grandma and Grandpa for a few days.

"Grandma, may I have a glass of water?" Justin asked.

I brought him the water.

A few minutes later he was back for more. "Grandma, may I have a glass of water?"

Once again I filled his glass.

Justin returned for a third glass, then a fourth. It was time to be a little suspicious as to where that water was going. "What are you doing with all that water, Justin?" I asked.

"Watering your flowers, Grandma," he answered proudly.

And so he was. Justin was busy, going throughout the house, pouring glasses of water into the vases of my *silk* flowers.

This *GRAND*-story comes to us by way of the author, Sylvia Bailey.

18

The Radio That Wouldn't Change Stations

by David Greenberg

Grandpa Sid and I had a great friendship. He would visit us nearly every weekend. My favorite "grandfather thing" was taking long drives with him to surprise destinations. It was not unusual for Grandpa Sid to come to the house and say something to me like: "Let's drive to Canada for the weekend! Leave your parents a note and tell them we'll call when we get there."

Even though the new highways were much faster, he would insist on using the old two-lane (no passing) roads so we could enjoy more time together. Those were wonderful times, and they remain wonderful memories.

As we drove along the road, Grandpa Sid would tell me countless stories about his childhood. He once told me a story about how, as a kid, he sometimes stretched money when it was in short supply. He would bore a hole in a nickel, and then tie a string through the hole so he could deposit it into the gas meter, then retrieve it by pulling on the string. A few extra hours of gas was a big thing.

One Sunday afternoon we were riding together in his brand new metallic silver Buick Electra 225, which happened to have a state-of-the-art AM/FM 8-track stereo/radio. Grandpa Sid made what he called a "pit stop," leaving the keys in the car so that I could listen to the radio.

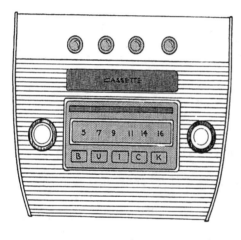

That radio was really special. It had huge, shiny chrome buttons that spelled the word "B-U-I-C-K." You pushed one of the buttons whenever you wanted to change the station. When I would press a button, the red needle would leap along the dial indicator to the pre-selected station.

I *loved* pushing those buttons.

Completely fascinated by the radio, I changed the station several times, then accidentally discovered that not only could I push the buttons in, but I could also pull them out. They worked both ways. This discovery excited me, and I pulled out *all* five buttons to see what would happen. At that moment Grandpa Sid returned, so I quickly pushed all the buttons back in and turned off the radio. We talked all the way home.

The next weekend Grandpa Sid came for another visit. He seemed upset about something; I eventually asked him what was wrong. He responded in a sort of agitated way, "I spent $100 and a whole day at the Buick dealership getting my radio fixed." (Now I wasn't exactly sure I was the cause of this problem, but I did remember the incident with the five buttons and figured I probably had *something* to do with it.)

Grandpa Sid went on to add, "That little red needle on the radio dial wouldn't move at all, so I took the car back to the dealer. No matter which button I pushed, the station never changed. The dealer thought the cable inside the radio had snapped; they had to take my whole dashboard apart to remove the radio."

"Really?" I said nervously.

"Really," responded Grandpa Sid. "When they finally got it out and checked the radio they found it wasn't broken at all. Someone, it seems, had set all the buttons to the same station! No matter which button I pushed, the station *never* changed!"

"Really?"

"Really," he repeated. Then Grandpa Sid gave me a big smile. I knew I didn't need to mention my part in the episode of *The Radio That Wouldn't Change Stations*. He knew! But, because he truly loved me, he never felt it necessary to place blame. In fact, we both enjoyed a good laugh (our secret) as we went for another of those long drives. You know, he even let me play with the radio the *whole* trip.

Anytime I feel like my personal needle is stuck, and I'm not moving, I just think about that episode with the radio. I know Grandpa Sid is smiling as he tells me, "Move on to another station, son. Play a new song."

David Greenberg is president of Atlanta-based, Simply Speaking, Inc. He is the author of *Thank God it's Monday! Designing a Life You Love Beyond the Weekend* (Goldleaf Publications, 1997).

19

Only a Dream

by Robert L. Bailey

One of the honors grandchildren bestow on their grandparents is their sincere desire to be around them and share the good times. And, it's even more special when they bring their friends along to spend some time with grandma and grandpa. At least that's the way it is under *normal* circumstances.

One of our grand-sons, Zack (then 5 years old), telephoned with the following message: "Grandpa, I had the neatest dream last night. I dreamed my whole class was staying over-night at *your* house. We were up real late, and making a lot of noise.

Grandpa, you got up and scolded us and made us go back to bed."

In a quick moment Zack added, "Grandpa, it was *great!*"

Now, according to Zack's mom, there are about 25 young-sters in that class. So, when you think about it, it really *was* great— great it was only a dream.

This story came to us by way of the author, Robert L. Bailey, an insurance company CEO and speaker from Ohio.

20

Grandpa's Secret

by Jim Moore

I had taken the day off from college to return home for my high school's biggest football game of the season. This particular game was much more than just a time of reunion; this game was even more than just the championship game of the Western Conference. This was *The Game*.

To top it all off, my father, Robert "Tut" Moore, coached one of the teams on the field. Believe me, when your career and the legacy you leave behind is evaluated on the number of wins and losses recorded by your team, each game is vitally important.

But this game was even more than all that; this game was the season! Even if your team was undefeated over the previous 10 games, lose *The Game* and your season would be considered a failure.

I'm sure you can imagine the tremendous pressure and stress felt by the entire family as the game moved into the final minutes of the last quarter. The score was tied with only 2 minutes remaining. Dad's team was driving toward the end zone. The very air in the stadium was thick and heavy with tension.

I couldn't handle sitting in the stands one moment longer. I observed my grandfather standing near the end zone (the one our team was marching toward). I took off to join him, running around and behind the grandstand. We stood there together and anxiously watched as our team, on three successive and unsuccessful plays, tried to score from the 1-yard line.

It was a nerve-racking, nail-biting time! When a time-out was called, I just couldn't stand it a moment longer. I *had* to have a cigarette (a habit I had only recently acquired). I looked at Grandpa. He was just as uptight as I was.

"I can't stand it, Grandpa, I've *got* to have a cigarette. Don't tell Grandma."

Grandpa looked relieved. He grinned, then pulled a pack of cigarettes from his pocket. "I won't tell if you won't tell," he said.

Jim Moore is founder and president of Moore Ideas, Inc. He is a professional speaker, author, and consultant specializing in performance and profit enhancement in retail operations.

21

Don't Worry

by LIBBYLOVE Griffin

Grandmother had been admitted to the hospital and would remain there for at least several days. Granddaughter was very eager to visit grandmother because Mama had agreed that she was now old enough to make the visit on her own. Granddaughter, wanting to be on her own but not necessarily alone, invited a friend to come along with her to the hospital.

Mama pulled up to the hospital entrance and the two girls left the car. The girls went up to Grandmother's room while Mama parked the car and walked back to the entrance. However, she did arrive in time to catch some of the conversation as she peeked into the room.

Grandmother was in a deep sleep. Mama heard her daughter lament, "This makes me so sad."

"What do you mean?" asked her friend. "She's probably just sleeping."

Granddaughter explained, "She looks so bad. How can you tell if she's sleeping?" To her friend she added, "I love my grandma, you know."

With great understanding, her girlfriend moved to stand next to her. Placing her arm around the concerned granddaughter, she extended these words of comfort: "Don't worry. You still have *another* one!"

LIBBYLOVE Griffin is the published author of two books, a professional speaker, and the mother of nine. She is "Granny Bibby" to 25 grandchildren and "Granny the Great" to three great-grandchildren.

22

Which One?

author unknown

A 10-year-old, under the tutelage of her grandmother, was becoming quite knowledgeable about the Bible.

Then, one day she floored her grandmother by asking this question: "Which virgin was the mother of Jesus: the Virgin Mary or the King James Virgin?"

Taken from the Web site for the *Foundation for Grandparenting*, and used with their kind permission. www.grandparenting.org

23

How Long?

by John Wooden

When I took my great-granddaughter, Lori Nicholson, shopping on her 11th birthday, the following conversation ensued as we reached the Northridge Mall:

"PaPa, I know it is hard for you to walk, and it's not fun to watch me shop, so please sit here on this bench and wait for me."

"That will be fine, honey."

"Good. Now don't worry about me. I can run, and I can yell, and I won't talk to strangers."

"Fine, honey. I'll wait for you right here. Don't rush; I will enjoy watching the people."

She returned after a while with some packages and said, "There are some other stores at the other end, and there are benches there where you can rest and wait."

We moved slowly down the mall until we reached the area where she wished to go. Then she said, "Sit here, PaPa. I won't be gone very long. Don't worry about me. I can run, and I can yell, and I won't talk to strangers. However, PaPa, I *do* need some more *money!*"

Some time after we had left the mall and were driving home, she said, "PaPa, how long are you going to live?"

"That's an odd question, honey," I replied. "I can't really answer that. People live longer today, and I've already outlived my parents by over 20 years. Why would you ask?"

"I hope you live a long, long time, PaPa, but at least for 5 more years."

"Why 5 years, Lori?" I questioned.

"Because I'm 11 today, and in 5 years I'll be 16. I want *you* to take me to get my driver's permit."

Basketball Hall of Famer John Wooden taught and coached at UCLA, where his basketball teams won a total of 10 NCAA national championships.

24

A Fine Mess This Is!

by Rosita Perez

"Out of the mouths of babes" has new meaning for me lately.

Lucas was 5 when he asked me, "Why do you use a cane, Grandma?"

I made the mistake many adults make; I over-explained.

43

"Well, Lucas," I said to my grandson, "I have a disease that's called 'MS.' That means I trip a lot. Remember when I fell down the stairs and broke my elbow? I don't want that to happen again, so I use a cane to help steady me as I walk."

He looked up at me with a scrunched-up face and one eye closed. He reminded me of the pirate in *Treasure Island* who uttered: "Ai! Me hearty!"

"You're a MESS?"

Obviously, that was what he heard.

Between pangs of convulsive laughter, I managed to say: "Yes, Lucas. Sometimes Grandma *is* a mess." No further explanation was given nor asked for. We both let it go at that.

This little lesson taught me to keep it simple, and not to make the mistake of thinking that, because I was heard, I was understood. The lesson has served me well in many situations since.

And my teacher was a 5-year-old boy.

Rosita Perez, BSW, CPAE is known as "The speaker who sings a different tune." A former social worker and mental health administrator, Rosita shares messages about *Challenges, Choices and Changes.*

25

"Peep"
by Mike Ditka

My granddaughter, Lauren Ashley Ditka, is 9 years old. She has always had a unique way of referring to me. Lauren calls me "Peep," a far cry from the more common "Grandpop," "Papaw," or "Granddad."

When she was a baby, Lauren would see me on TV when her parents would point me out on the screen. I suppose she was trying to say "TV," but it always came out "Peep." The name stuck, and is still with me today.

She's quite a young lady. Recently she told me this joke:

Question: *Why did the coach go to the bank?*

Answer: *To get his quarterback!*

Mike Ditka is the head coach of the New Orleans Saints. (And the Texas publisher of *GRAND-Stories* recalls that, among many distinctions, Mike once played tight end for the Dallas Cowboys during the Tom Landry era.)

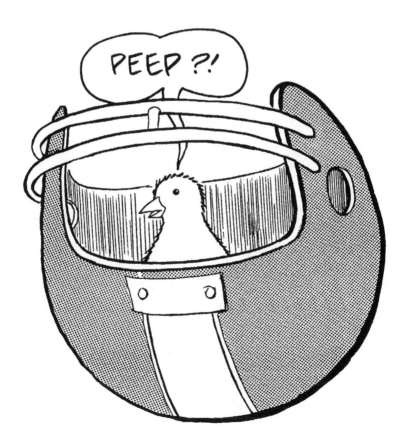

26

A Scary Noise

by Barbara Fenter

When my granddaughter, Allison, was just 3-and-a-half years old, she came to spend the night with me. My husband (her grandfather) was out of town, so it was an opportunity for the two of us to spend some time together. When it was time for Allison to go to bed, we agreed to keep the doors to our bedrooms open so that I could hear her if she needed me.

In the morning I was awakened by a rather strange noise. It was a very soft, but persistent, plunk, plunk sound coming from the piano in the living room. I thought I'd better check it out.

I found Allison at the piano. She was striking the keys in an effort to send me a wake-up call. I walked into the room.

"Allison, Honey," I asked, "why didn't you just come in and wake me?"

"Well, Grandma," replied Allison, "I *was* coming, but I heard this scary noise coming from your room." She paused for a moment, and then exclaimed, "I thought there was a pig in there!"

Obviously Grandpa was right all along; I am a snoring woman.

Barbara Fenter is a homemaker from Ohio and grandmother of four. She teams with a partner to speak in area schools concerning depression and suicide awareness.

27

"I'll Take a Baggie"
by Sharlene Zwing

One day I was busy fixing my daughter a sandwich for her school lunch.

"Mommy, can I have my sandwich wrapped in foil instead of in a baggie?" she asked.

"Why?"

"Because everyone is recycling foil at my school," she replied.

My husband quickly joined in the conversation, "Your mom doesn't like to use foil because she heard that foil might cause Alzheimer's."

"Is that how Grandpa got Old-Timers?" my daughter asked. "I'm not ready for that. I'll take a baggie."

Sharlene Zwing partners Zwing Advertising with her husband Ron, and also writes a "local" column in the Myrtle Beach Herald. She is the mother of four children.

28

A Not-Too-Happy Little Girl
by Susan Stephani Hitchler

When our first grandchild, Jamie Marie Hitchler, was just 2 years old, her grandpa and I took her to our nephew's birthday party. The bad news was that we had to travel at least 2 hours from our home to the place of the party—and return. The good news was that they had a swimming pool, an inviting in-ground pool, ready for jumping and splashing.

Jamie had a truly wonderful day. She played, then played some more. She loved being in the pool with her grandma and the rest of the "kids." She ate lots of good food (not especially good for her—just good). She played with everything; an exciting, fun-filled day.

By the time we were ready to leave for home, Jamie had reached the stage we call "overtired"—an understatement at best. She was placed in her car seat in the back of the car.

She wasn't a happy camper, but we hoped that, as soon as we were on our way, she would fall asleep. No such luck! Jamie fussed and cried and was just plain crabby.

Really crabby! The child was exhausted all right, but she was also too overstimulated to give in to even a moment of sleep.

We finally compromised with her as I heeded her insistent pleas to come into the back seat and sit beside her. My job was to console; I tried my best. She was sobbing as I put my arm around and spoke what I intended to be these comforting words: "Jamie; everything will be okay. Jamie, you're such a *happy* girl."

When I made that last comment, about her being a happy girl, she turned to look at me with eyes wide open—in total disbelief. She couldn't fathom what she had just heard me say!

Little Jamie looked me right in the eye. She pointed one of her chubby little fingers toward her face, indicating the flowing tears. "But Gramma, I'm NOT happy; I'm CRYING!

Poor thing, she was probably thinking about being stuck with a grandma who was not too bright.

Oh well, there's always Grandpa.

Susan Stephani Hitchler is a professional speaker, consultant and grandma.

48

29

When is Old — OLD?

by Ernie Wendell

It's playtime! Grandpa and granddaughter are enjoying each other's company. It just doesn't get any better.

This game is called "Jump and Catch and Twirl Around." It works like this: The little granddaughter climbs to the third step of the stairs separating the den from the next level of the house. She stands there for a moment, arms spread out like angel wings, and then she jumps into the air space separating her from her grandpa. Grandpa makes the catch and twirls the little girl around and around.

Pure accelerated joy; excited laughter fills the room. A safe landing is achieved. Then it's up the stairs to do it once again, and then again.

After half a dozen jumps and catches, Grandpa is having a little problem with his breathing; it is labored and insufficient. He holds his hand up in the air (the same signal one uses for stopping traffic).

"Hold everything," he gasps. "I need to take a break to catch my breath."

The granddaughter will have none of it. "Oh, Grandpa," she implores, "come on; just one more time. Please?" (It's always, "One more time.")

"Honey, you don't understand," pants the Winded One. "Your Grandpa is tired. He needs a rest. I'm getting old!"

A look of genuine concern covers her face. She is still—no movement at all. Then, she slowly places one hand on each hip and angles her blonde-covered head back so she can better see her partner-in-play.

She gazes up at her grandpa with wide blue eyes. She has thought the situation through. With the wisdom and understanding of a child in search of a quick solution to her problem, she declares: "You are NOT old, Grandpa; you just LOOK old!"

Ernie Wendell is the compiler of *GRAND-Stories*. Ernie is an inspirational speaker and seminar leader. He is the author of the book, *Stepping Stones to* Success (Milestone Publications, 1997).

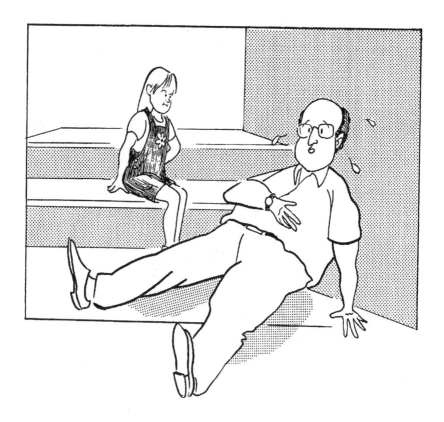

30

A Picky Problem

by Lois Blanton

My mother took our 4-year-old son on an outing. She was introducing Tim to a new experience —picking blueberries.

After an hour or so of picking berries, Tim told his grandmother that he had to go pee. She advised that it was perfectly alright to do it right there in the woods.

He took a lot of convincing. She insisted and persisted. Finally, when he couldn't wait any longer—he did it. However, when Tim had finished he was once again upset. He cried because Grandma wouldn't take him home so he could wash his hands!

Lois Blanton is a mother and grandmother. She is also the secretary to the Dean of the Divinity School at Duke University (Durham, North Carolina).

31

The Big Switch

by Wayne E. Baughman

Kate Smith was truly one of America's favorite entertainers. She was a wonderful singer (*God Bless America* and *When The Moon Comes Over The Mountain*), and, for a long time, she hosted a variety show on TV. It was one of my grandpa's favorite television shows. He really enjoyed watching and hearing Kate belt out a song.

One afternoon my grandfather was totally engrossed in watching *The Kate Smith Show*. My brother, Dick, who was about 3 years old at the time, entered the room and walked right up to the television set. With his hands firmly planted on his hips, Dick faced my grandfather and said, "Me no like Kate Miff!" And with that he switched off the TV.

My grandfather sat straight up in his chair. He got to his feet, walked to the set, and, without saying a word, he switched the set back on. No sooner had he sat back down when his persistent little grandson was right back at the set again, switching it off.

"No Kate Miff!" he exclaimed. So back and forth they went, Dick and Grandpa, turning the set on and off.

When the show was over, I'm pretty sure Grandpa hadn't seen much of it. But no matter; he and 3-year-old Dick were having a laughing good time enjoying each other and the magic of the moment. My grandpa's good nature made that moment possible (and many other moments as well).

From that day on, my grandfather always made certain that Dick was occupied with something else so he could watch "Kate Miff" in peace.

Wayne E. Baughman's business, Creative Presentations, assists people in controlling the fear of speaking and helps them to make better business presentations and to be more creative.

32

Grandma's Job Description

by John Carroll

When she was 6 years old, Erynn, our daughter had the world just about figured out.

One evening, as her mother was reading to her, I happened to wander into the room.

I listened as Lori read from *The Secret Garden*, the classic children's tale about a little British girl who had spent her early years among the aristocracy in the then British colony of India. During those first years the little girl had enjoyed the convenience and comfort of an "ayah," a maidservant whose job it was to do the bidding of even the youngest child.

The term "ayah" was not familiar to me. I decided to check Erynn's listening and understanding skills. So I asked her, "What does that word 'ayah' mean, Erynn?"

Taking only a moment she replied, "It means someone who does *everything* for you."

"Do you mean like a nanny?" I questioned, perhaps looking a bit perplexed.

Lori entered our conversation with, "No, an ayah is not a nanny." Looking up from the book, my wife added, "An ayah is more of a servant who really does whatever the child asks."

"Yes, Daddy," Erynn then chimed. "You know—just like *Grandma!*"

Erynn's daddy, John Carroll, is president of Unlimited Performance in Mt. Pleasant, South Carolina. He specializes in organizational and individual performance information. jcarroll@uperform.com.

33

Mr. Smarty Pants and Grandma

by Connie Alderman

The first thing little Tony did when he arrived at Grandma's house was to take a flying leap onto the sofa. "Tony," Grandma asked, "I guess you weren't listening the last time you were here when I told you not to jump on the furniture."

Tony giggled, then ran to hide in the closet (knocking down the vacuum cleaner and a coat in the process).

"Oh, oh," said Grandma. "It looks like Mr. Smarty Pants is here." (Mr. Smarty Pants was usually the culprit when things went wrong; their mutual understanding.) "You know what he's like," she added.

Tony put his thumbs in the corners of his mouth, pulled his lower eyelids down, and stuck out his tongue. He knew!

"I wonder where Mr. Smarty Pants comes from?" Grandma mused as she sat down on the sofa and held out her arms as an invitation to Tony.

"He comes from inside of me," Tony said, climbing up on her lap. "He's got little things on top of his head, and a tail too." He was getting excited and talking faster. "And he carries a pointy thing. And you know what, Grandma? He plays football."

"He plays football?" asked Grandma. She was puzzled.

"Yes, I see him on signs. He's all red!"

Now Grandma understood. "Oh, you mean the ASU Sun Devils," she offered with a smile. "Well, Tony," she continued, "don't you think Mr. Smarty Pants makes a lot of trouble for you? Tony's head nodded up and down. "What do you think we can do about that?" she inquired.

Tony's eyes searched the ceiling for an answer. "Keep him inside me?"

"How can you do that?"

"Build a brick wall. You know, like the *Three Little Pigs* did," Tony proudly boasted.

"But if you did that, Tony, nothing could get in either."

"Like what?" Tony wanted to know.

"Like love," Grandma responded, smoothing and caressing his hair.

"Hmmm ... I'll have to think about that." Tony slid off her lap and hurried to ask, "Can we play a game now?" Grandma opened the desk drawer and Tony reached for a deck of cards. "Bet I can beat you!" he said.

"Grandma, I know what to do about Mr. Smarty Pants," Tony announced, even before the game was over.

"Oh? What? Tell me!"

"I'll build the wall out of marshmallows. Then love can still get in."

"Well, what about Mr. Smarty Pants?" asked Grandma.

"Um, he's trying to tear down the wall."

"What's he doing with the marshmallows, Tony?"

"He's piling them up in my heart. I can give them to other people." Tony folded his arms and smiled smugly. As far as he was concerned, the problem was solved.

"Little puffs of love. How sweet. Get it, Tony? Marsh-mallows ... sweet ...?" Grandma smiled and hugged him. Tony felt great.

Then Grandma glanced at her watch; she jumped up. "Tony, I'm late for an appointment. We'll have to hurry!" They rushed to the car, buckled up, and off they went.

"Grandma," remarked Tony, straining to see the speedometer, "you're going over 40."

"I'm late, Tony," she mumbled, feebly excusing her excessive speed. "Why did I ever explain speedometers and traffic signs to him?" she wondered. She glanced in her rear view mirror and saw flashing red and blue lights coming up behind her.

"Oh, oh," Grandma groaned, knowing that now she was going to be even later. She pulled over to the side of the road.

The policeman approached the car and spoke to Grandma. "I'm sorry, lady, but I'm going to give you a ticket for speeding. You were going faster than the speed limit." He was very stern.

"It's not her fault," Tony blurted out to the policeman. "Her Mrs. Smarty Pants just got out."

The officer looked puzzled. "I told her, but she wouldn't listen," Tony continued.

Grandma smiled, but Tony thought she didn't look too happy when the policeman started writing the ticket. She took it from the officer, thanked him as she put it in her purse, and drove away ... slowly.

"Maybe you should have given him a marshmallow," Tony suggested.

Connie Alderman is an entertainer, humorist, writer and composer/lyricist. She began her career at the age of 50, and says life is good at every age. www.doitnow.com

34

Pea Patch Predicament

by Al Walker

For two weeks every summer, I visited my grandparents on their dairy farm in Edgefield, South Carolina. It was always dark when we got up every morning, even in the summertime, because we had to be at the barn milking by sun-up. One of those mornings, Pop told me we were going to finish milking, plant some peas, then go fishing.

That got me excited. There was nothing I loved to do more than go fishing with my grandfather.

Pop had a rule: He never used the tractor to work any crop if folks were going to be eating what came out of that plot. It was alright to use the tractor to work corn or hay for the cows, but for anything humans consumed, he didn't want gasoline or oil anywhere near it. So we hitched up an old mule named Betsy to the plow, grabbed a sack of pea seed, and headed for the field.

When we got there, Pop told me to stand by the edge of the plot when he started plowing. After he'd cut a few rows, he stopped the mule, tied the plow lines around the handle, and walked back over to me.

"Here's where you come in," he said, handing me a relatively small sack of pea seed. He showed me how to take two or three pea seeds, drop them in the ground at the beginning of the row, pat some dirt over the top of them with a foot, drop two or three more, step on them, and continue that process up and down each row.

"Remember, when we get through planting these peas, we're going fishing," he said with a big grin. Pop knew that would make me work harder, because he knew how much I loved to fish.

So I started planting peas under that hot, South Carolina sun. After a few rows it didn't seem like my sack of seed was getting *any* smaller. I figured that if I didn't do something, it would take the rest of the day to plant all those peas (no fishing). I decided the only solution to the problem was to eat a few of the pea seeds. And that's what I did.

I worked myself up to one-for-one; for every seed I'd put in the ground, I'd pop one in my mouth. At that rate I finished pretty quickly.

"Pop, I'm through; we can go fishing now," I hollered.

He stopped the mule and looked over at me. There was confusion and concern on his face. Without saying a word, he started walking over to me.

Something told me I was in trouble. He picked up the empty sack, shook it out, and kicked around in the dirt to see if I'd planted too many.

"Son, what did you do with the pea seed?"

"Uh ... Pop, I ate a few." (I couldn't come up with a good lie, or I would have tried it.)

To this day, I'll never forget the expression on his face or what he said to me. "My word, son," Pop chuckled, "One of these days you're gonna swell up and be as big as a barn."

He was right. I did grow up to be a big, ol' boy—about the size of at least a *small* barn (tipping the scales at a little under 400 pounds at 6 feet, 1 inch tall).

Al Walker is a professional speaker whose humor and powerful message has kept audiences laughing for over 20 years. He's known as "a big man with a big message." Anyone who has ever seen and heard him agrees.

35

A Bad Haircut

by Marilyn Redmond

My daughter Janet was making her haircut disaster known to all who would listen.

"I got butchered at the beauty shop," she lamented. "I'm so upset; I don't want anyone to see me like this. It's terrible! Too short—just awful! I want to hide somewhere and never come out."

About that time one of my twin grandsons, Robert, raised a question: "Mom, don't you wash your hair every day when you shower?"

"Yes, but what does that have to do with this awful haircut?"

"Well, Mom," added Ryan, the other grandson, "When you water the flowers every day, they grow faster."

Marilyn Redmond is a registered counselor and professional speaker from Boise, Idaho. www.tcmnet.com/~angelart

36

The Sperrys

by Winnie Shows

In the living room,
Grandpa strides in with ceremony,
Removes his jacket,
Sits with purpose in his favorite chair
And calls us to worship.
We gather from all corners and listen,
Eager for the miracle to happen again.
He solemnly opens his wallet
And reaches in to the holy of holies
Like a priest at his altar,
Extracting a single dollar-bill.
He looks at it lovingly,
Caresses it reverently,
Elevates it like a sacrament.

The hosannas of anticipation

Dance in my eyes.

He blesses me with it,

And I accept it humbly,

My thank-yous rising like incense

As he glows in happiness,

Feeling divine.

In the kitchen,

Fingering her rosary beads

Beneath a picture of the Sacred Heart,

Grandma slips me a five.

"Don't tell your grandpa," she whispers.

Winnie Shows is a speaker and consultant from Menlo Park, California, and author of *Hairball and Other Poems of Transformation* (Shows, 1999). www.wshows.com

37

A 4-Year-Old Genius

by Charlene M. Rice

My 4-year-old granddaughter, Lauren, had already learned to operate a television set. She could also insert and rewind video tapes in the VCR. Pondering, I thought of the access she had to all the new ideas. Her mom and dad owned a 53-inch color television and a word processor. I knew that her grandfather owned four computers and a fax machine. When she visited my house, I would see her at the computer playing games.

One day, as Lauren and I were driving down the highway on our way to get the mail, my heart and soul were filled with love for my sweet little granddaugher.

"Lauren," I asked, "do you know that you are blessed? You have a big, color TV, a fax machine, and a computer. Isn't that wonderful? Just think, when I was growing up, all I had was a little radio."

With my heart so full of love, I smiled as I kept on driving. There were a few moments of silence.

"Mamaw?" she then asked.

"Yes, Darling?"

"Is that why you're so DUMB?"

Charlene M. Rice writes humorous poems and stories relating to chaotic situations that occur in daily life. She and her husband own a furniture store in Poteet, Texas. Daily contact with the public gives Charlene a strong insight into human emotions.

<u>38</u>

Enjoying the Unexpected
by Mary Murray Shelton

On a summer's evening over 30 years ago, I sat with my family in the kitchen of my cousin's home. We were all seated around the kitchen table preparing to eat a wonderful meal of fried chicken, mashed potatoes, salad, bread, and corn on the cob. My aunt, a proud first-time grandma, was there too, sitting next to Cara, her 2-year-old granddaughter.

The good food and balmy evening made for animated conversation. As we chatted our way through the meal, Cara ate her corn with great enthusiasm and somewhat messy results. We all commented on how cute it was to watch her as she struggled with, and enjoyed to the last morsel, that fresh corn.

Before long, Cara had finished her corn and looked around the table, smiling at the rest of us. Suddenly, she affectionately put her little head on her grandmother's shoulder. We all smiled at the sweetness of her action, commenting with variations on "Aw ... isn't that cute?"

Cara leaned on past her grandmother, lifted Grandma's corn right off her plate, sat up again, and began to eat it. Her grandmother burst into laughter at this cute trick, and so did the rest of us.

Cara beamed at us with her butter and corn kernel-covered face, pleased that she had amused us. Although I was only about 9 at the time, I have never forgotten that meal or the fullness of our laughter. It has seemed to me ever since that the heart of grandparenting must be made up of moments like this.

The Reverend Mary Murray Shelton is an ordained minister of 13 years in the United Church of Religious Science. She is presently writing a book, *Guidance from the Darkness*.

Part Two

Faith and Courage

T hese stories show us that, although life can sometimes be tough, the human spirit is much tougher.

39

The Second Time Around
by JMB

Sometimes it's necessary for grandparents to rise above personal needs and wants and become parents again. It isn't that they want to re-assume that role; not at all. They do it for the sake of their grandkids.

Addiction to drugs robbed my daughter and her husband from being good and decent parents. Their neglect made it imperative that my husband and I take custody of our two grandchildren. We promised the parents that, if they would get clean and stay sober, we would one day, with ceremony, celebrate the return of their children to them.

At first the parents lied so much we couldn't believe them. But then things gradually began to change. The first sign of "clean" thinking came when they stopped blaming everyone and everything for their problems and troubles.

They began driving their car *legally*. For the first time, the car was insured, displayed proper license tags, and even had an emission sticker. Eventually they found a place to live, and they weren't evicted. We also noticed other changes. They would show up on time, looking bright-eyed and healthier.

We scheduled a Re-Connection Ceremony at our church on Father's Day, 3-and-a-half years after we had taken the grandchildren into our home. We were all dressed up and standing at the altar, the grandkids next to their grandparents, and the parents on the other side of the aisle.

Our pastor spoke of the Prodigal Son and the joy of reunion. He then handed a candle to our eldest grandchild, who carried it to his mom and dad. He stood with them as the altar flowers were given to our youngest grandchild. She presented them to me, then crossed over the aisle to join her parents and her brother.

At the end of this very special service we all hugged and cried. There was complete and genuine forgiveness all around. That afternoon our grandchildren and their parents went home as a family.

Several months later, things were going well enough that I decided to redecorate the grandkids' bedrooms. When the eldest grandchild heard of it, he asked if I would just keep them the same—for when they came to visit. That's what I did.

It's now been 8 years. The parents are still together. They're still sober, and they now have a third child. My husband and I count our blessings; we are grateful for the relationship we have with *all* of them.

Now we love just being grandparents.

(Author's name withheld for the sake of the family.)

40

Grandpa's Good Advice

by Stephen Robbins Yarnall

His name was Colonel Charles Burton Robbins. To me he was Bompy, my maternal grandfather. I still have memories of a visit with him at his summer cabin in the Iowa woods. I was 6.

Bompy was a quiet, good-humored, kindly, gray-haired grandfather whose casual ways belied his considerable wisdom and experience. His collection of weapons from the Spanish-American War and World War I was an awesome sight. It made a lasting impression on a young boy.

That summer visit was really special because we were alone, just the two of us at his backwoods cabin. The experience took on even greater proportion when, after a bit of begging on my part, Bompy let me ride his horse around the cabin area.

He told me to be careful, not to go too far, and not to get lost. But he also gave me some advice in case I *did* get lost. "Just let go of the reins and the horse will bring you home," he said.

Off I went down the cool and inviting trail. I came to a large open meadow. After riding around in the meadow, enjoying every minute of my new freedom, I decided it was time to head for home. But, as fate would have it, I couldn't find the trail. On the fringe of panic, I searched the border of the meadow. It was covered all the way around; trees, trees, and more trees.

There was no opening *anywhere*.

I then remembered Bompy's advice: "Just let go of the reins and the horse will bring you home." Well, I did—and he did!

I have never forgotten that good, loving advice. On numerous occasions I have had reason to use it again and again. Indeed, there are those times when one should let go of the reins and be shown the way home.

Dr. Stephen R. Yarnall is a practicing cardiologist and internal medicine specialist in Edmonds, Washington. He is a popular speaker and may be reached at (425) 744-1780. yarnall@gte.net

41

Standing Tall

by Marcia Reynolds

My grandmother stood all of 4 feet, 10 inches tall in her stocking feet. She was the very first adult I could look down on, although I never grew taller than 5 feet myself. She made *me* feel tall. Her meager height, however, didn't come anywhere close to representing her stature. Those who knew her well would have considered her to be taller and braver than most men.

My grandmother was only 13 years old, and my grandfather 14, when they were married in the Ukrainian region of Russia. They both came from families of successful Jewish merchants. In those days (the early 1900s) any merchant in Russia was considered a Capitalist (*not* a good thing) and was damned by the Bolsheviks. Jewish merchants were considered to be worse and carried an even blacker mark against them.

The Bolshevik Revolution erupted throughout the land. Only 2 years after their marriage, my grandparents escaped Russia in order to save their lives. They left their families behind—forever.

They enjoyed the safety and the security of living in the United States. They had five children, all sons. My grandfather contracted a lung disease, and it became primarily my grandmother's responsibility to raise the family. For more than 20 years, she worked in the same sandwich shop until they moved to Arizona. All her boys grew up to be successful businessmen.

I was able to spend many weekends with her as I grew up. I would often sit and listen as she told me stories of her beautiful sisters. I never realized, at least not until I was in my teens, that she never knew what happened to her sisters after she and my grandfather fled Russia. Occasionally, while talking about such things, tears would well up in her eyes. She would then stand up, put her hand over her heart, look up toward the sky and say, "God bless America."

She always said it with such conviction. For some reason I always felt a little funny whenever she did that—not because I didn't love my country, but because I never quite felt that same depth of feeling. And, I guess, I always felt a little guilty for not joining her. Afterwards, she would sit back down and resume her storytelling.

As a college graduation present, my father gave me a trip to Israel. I hadn't even been out of the country before, except one time when I visited a Mexican border town (which doesn't really count for much in cultural appreciation). That trip to Israel enabled me to feel even closer to my grandmother. The sights were truly incredible; being in Jerusalem aroused the very depths of my emotions. I found the people to be interesting and fun. Yet, that year, like most years, the people of Israel and Palestine were killing each other. Three times while we were there, I visited cities that were bombed by the Palestinians the very next day. For the first time in my life, I felt truly unsafe, kind of compromised.

In retrospect, I loved my trip to Israel. But even more I loved stepping into the airplane that was to bring me home. I will never forget the wave of emotion that washed over me at the first glimpse of the mountains that surround the city where I live.

I sensed my grandmother's presence as we descended and broke through the clouds. She was no longer alive, but somehow I felt her standing next to me. I stood up, placed my hand over my heart, and said, "God bless America."

Three other passengers said, "Amen."

I remember my little grandmother. I remember her every time I express my gratitude for the life I've been so lucky to lead. I hope that someday I can stand just as tall as she did.

Marcia Reynolds, MA, MEd, is president of *Covisioning*. She provides personal coaching, speaks at conferences, and leads seminars on being successful while maintaining a quality of life.

42

To My Grandfather

by David Ryback

We never met. How could we? You were killed in the Holocaust along with so many others. Yet, by way of a single photograph, a picture of you that my mother (your daughter) showed me over and over again, I feel that you have been there for me—always.

It's not just the photograph, which would have been sufficient in itself; it's your soft, loving eyes, the youthfulness of your trimmed beard, and all those letters you wrote to my mother from the "old country." Those letters expressed your concerns for her welfare and all the uncertainties of a new life in America.

I wonder; how does a loving parent let go of a 19-year-old innocent and naive daughter, and find the will to permit her to cross an ocean? It was a separation so wide that eternity marked the time of your next meeting.

Did you know, deep down in your soul, what would have happened had she stayed? Did you feel in your fatherly bones that severing her from your presence (but never from your heart) in that time and place would allow her to pursue a full and free life somewhere else? Did you know it would free her from what destroyed so many others?

Until this moment, Grandfather, I have never speculated on how you met your death. Does it really matter? Regardless of the circumstances, I know it was ruthless and senseless. I'm convinced that you were one of those who, early on, gave your life to protect the lives of others. And I know, with conviction, that your actions would make me proud. In that single photo, I saw it all in your eyes. Had you survived, Grandfather, I know you would have been there for my youth, and I would have lived better and suffered less.

Your daughter (my mother), and the many millions just like her, suffered the loss of their loved ones to a merciless genocide. How did they do it? Perhaps, in some spiritual way, they refused to give up what had been ripped away from them so incomprehensibly. To them, you somehow continued to live.

Grandfather, let me tell you what has happened. Your daughter, the youngest in your family (the "Jesus" baby, as she was known), married Isaac, the man who had sent for her. He did not take the sort of care for her you would have liked. Isaac was in and out of several small businesses, and she shared in all those problems.

They operated a small general store in a rough part of town where drinking and rowdiness were commonplace. It was mother's "school" for learning the ways of America. Soon she became pregnant with her first child, a boy. It was a wonder she could cope; she was barely out of her teens. Coming from your loving and protective home did not prepare her for the rigors of life.

But life does have a way of working out well after all. She and Isaac managed to raise four healthy children—two boys, two girls. You can be proud of each of your grandchildren.

I have missed you; I believe we all have. It's strange, Grandfather, but there has been little thought of Isaac's parents, the *other* grandparents. Nor was there ever much said of your wife, our mother's mother.

We must have been influenced by those letters you wrote to your daughter. We could see the words and appreciate the penmanship. The written word is powerful, and your letters drew us to you. Imagine; the pen you held touched the paper we held, linking us together. That bond spanned an ocean and connected two continents; it spanned generations and connected hearts; it spanned death and connected souls.

Isaac died some years ago. Your daughter remarried, and now lives contentedly in Israel. She truly loves the country of our ancestors, Grandfather, and she feels deeply that she belongs there. But her children are Americans; they remain here.

We have not told our mother that my brother (her eldest son) is very ill and not expected to live much longer. I do not wish to withhold this bad news from our mother, but it is a family consensus and I agree to it for now. I will see her soon. I will not lie to her; my words of heartbreaking reality will likely only confirm what she already senses and suspects. How can a mother not know about her child when all around her already know?

I want to experience the comfort of your presence when I tell her. Death is simple; a passing. Why should we fear it; I don't, for I know you'll be there to greet us. A life that loves truth can accept death and separation.

Your letters to my mother were lovingly written and lovingly cherished. They have taught me that love transcends distance, absence, and time. I lean on the memory of your words and hold to their truth in my life.

David Ryback is a speaker and consultant living in Atlanta, Georgia. He is the author of *Putting Emotional Intelligence to Work* (Butterworth-Heinemann, 1997). (404) 377-3588. docryback@aol.com

43

Quick Action

by Ernie Wendell

In the late 1800s, my great-grandmother Margaret (we called her "Little Grandma") arrived at Ellis Island, the gateway to opportunity. She and her family of nine had made the epic journey from Germany eagerly searching for a new beginning in the New World, the United States of America.

The Ivo family gathered with the other newly arrived immigrants; their assembly filled the arrival building to overflowing. They all waited in anticipation, wondering what would happen next.

Language was definitely a barrier to understanding; confusion ruled the day. Eventually the Ivos came to understand that they were to line up so that the medical doctor could give each of them the required physical examination. The family lined up according to age and status: Otto, Amanda, Walter, Richard, Hans, Emma, and Karl with my great-grandfather and great-grandmother at the head.

The inspecting doctor, with a look here and a touch there, made his way down the Ivo line-up. He moved from one to the next, and at each one he nodded and smiled, indicating approval. And then he arrived in front of my great-uncle Karl (the youngest) at the end of the line. This time, however, he did not nod or smile. Instead, the doctor carefully examined Karl's left eye.

The pupil in Karl's eye was not normal and round; it was broken and ran in an irregular line from the center to the lower part of the eye. The doctor studied Karl for what to my great-grandmother seemed a very long time. Then he took a large white tag from his pocket, wrote something on it, and hung the tag over the boy's neck. He then moved on to the next group of immigrants.

Little Grandma Ivo did not have any idea what the doctor had written on the tag around Karl's neck, but she didn't like it. She sensed it was *not* a good thing.

What to do? Well, just as soon as the doctor was out of sight she rushed over to Karl and jerked that tag from around his neck. She quickly crumpled it into a small ball and tossed it into a nearby trash heap. Nothing was going to impede *their* journey, and nothing was going to keep them from entering this new land. No one was going to be left behind.

And that was that. She instructed her family, in no uncertain way, to follow her. They calmly marched out of the building and into the free air of America. Shortly thereafter they boarded a train for Chicago where they established a new home.

My great-grandmother Ivo never looked back on her quick action. Her bravery and resourcefulness in the face of adversity was a story told and retold. No one ever questioned what she did—the right or wrong of it. It was just something a mother would do.

My great-uncle Karl? He enjoyed a wonderful and prosperous life in these United States. His first wife, Elva, died when he was about 65. They had no children. Karl then married a young woman (in her 20s, as I recall), and they had four children. He lived to see all his children grow to adulthood.

I'm so glad Little Grandma pulled off that tag.

Ernie Wendell is the compiler of *GRAND-Stories*. Ernie is an inspirational keynote speaker, seminar leader and author of the book, *Stepping Stones to Success* (Milestone Publications, 1997).

44

A Little Growing Up

by Nan Andrews Amish

I was my grandmother Mamie's first and favorite granddaughter. I could do no wrong in her eyes; she always thought I was the best. During my growing up years, she was my constant hero and my ultimate source of unconditional love.

For some reason Mamie did not treat my mother as kindly and lovingly as she treated me. My mother was definitely *not* the favorite child. That was a slot reserved for my uncle, her brother. He was known to take advantage of his special status at times, and he could be less than honest about his motives.

After I was grown, my uncle once told my grandmother that my mother was being manipulative, attempting to get at him through me. He probably used the comment defensively to respond to something my grandmother had asked; I'm not certain. But I did know that my mother was *not* involved, nor was she manipulative in any way. I wanted my grandmother to know the truth.

I decided to tell Mamie the facts as I knew them. I told her that her daughter was not involved in any way, that it was her son who had created and colored a story to suit his purposes. Although I needed to defend my mother, I knew there was a risk in doing so. Mamie wasn't going to like hearing any disparaging remarks about her favorite child. It could have changed forever my relationship with my grandmother.

I took the risk. I found our love to be strong, and unconditional love to be even stronger. Mamie listened and heard me, even though I told her something about her son she really didn't want to hear. She apologized for my uncle's conduct, forgave him for being human, and approved of the way I had supported my mother.

I think we all grew a little that day. I know I did.

When Mamie died years later, I was blessed knowing we were at peace with each other. No regrets—nothing left unsaid. It's true; the truth *will* set you free; and love is forever.

Nan Andrews Amish, MBA, is a professional speaker, consultant, and coach. She specializes in leadership and organizational effectiveness. (800) 858-1750.

45

Just a Coincidence?

by Fire "Captain Bob" Smith

We had one grandchild and we were expecting another at any moment. It was a time of great concern, for more reasons than one.

I was heading toward the telephone to call our son Rob, his wife Nancy, and our grandson, Trevor. We needed to know how they were doing. It was Tuesday morning and a television news reporter had just provided some on-site details of the Russian River rising to flood stage. The Russian River was just a block from their home in Guerneville, California. We feared for the safety of our children.

Before I reached the phone it rang. I instinctively knew it was Nancy. I put the receiver to my ear, and, before I could say anything, she spoke.

"Dad? Rob and I need your help—*fast!*"

How bad is it?" I asked. (My 25 years as a firefighter were taking over automatically). "Is Rob there now?"

"Yes," Nancy replied, "but only because I'm so scared. He was on call at the Firehouse, but I called him home. I'm concerned for Trevor and the baby."

She went on to explain the situation. "We've moved all our valuables to the highest point in the attic, and we've taken all we could from the first floor and moved it to the second."

Nancy paused for a long moment. "Dad, the river exceeded the 34-foot flood stage on Monday morning. It's still raining today."

Sixteen inches of rain had already fallen. They were without electricity, water, and heat. Water from the river had already come through the front door, and it was now edging up to the second step of the stairway. The new prediction: a rise to 48 feet.

The baby was scheduled to arrive on Thursday—in *2* days. It was time to get her out of there!

I informed Nancy that they were evacuating folks by Army Reserve helicopters. "There is absolutely no way I'm leaving by helicopter," she responded. "Boat, yes; helicopter, NO!" She had made up her mind. I could easily have pushed the crisis button into a "Code Three" adrenaline rush.

But I had been working on accepting life as it is—on life's terms. I didn't panic. After the call, my wife Harriet and I prayed a simple prayer: "Lord, keep our babies safe, and take us to them."

A feeling of peace and calm came over us. We packed some things and headed out in search of our loved ones. Some of the folks already evacuated had been taken to Sebastabol, so we headed in that direction.

Traffic slowed to a standstill as we approached Sebastabol. A UPS driver was advising motorists to turn left at the intersection to avoid the traffic snarl. About a mile down that side road, we passed a firehouse. Perhaps they would know what was going on; we turned back to check.

Once inside the firehouse we saw a fellow firefighter, Bruno Brungardt (Bruno and I work together at the fire department.). He had some information: "I just heard on the Guerneville radio channel that they were taking a pregnant woman to the bridge by Zodiac boat, then out by helicopter."

We thanked Bruno, returned to the road, then, on a chance that it might be our girl, we headed for the Sonoma County Airport. "Right, Nancy, absolutely no way you were going out by helicopter?" I thought. It was getting darker by the minute, but the road to the airport was still open.

When we arrived, I inquired about the helicopter flights. They had been canceled due to darkness and lightening. "Where have they taken those who were brought in?" I questioned.

"In town—to Veterans Hall."

"Are any of the evacuees still there?"

"Maybe."

"Could any of them be at the airport fire station?" I asked.

"Maybe." We drove over to the firehouse.

As we stepped out of our van, a strange feeling, an aura, came over me. Something significant was about to happen. Life seemed to go into slow motion as we ducked under a partially rolled up rear door.

A big army sergeant turned to look at us; he was holding our 2-year-old grandson in his arms. About that time, our son Rob looked up from an open duffel bag, and Nancy walked in from the other room. They looked like drowned rats, but they looked plenty good to us. We all just stood there in a moment of disbelief.

"Do you know these people?" the sergeant asked Trevor.

"Yeah," our grandson answered him in a high whisper.

They had arrived on the last flight out, in a huge Army Reserve Chinook helicopter. There was no way we could have planned the events that brought us together. It was unbelievable. The only answer we can accept is that a simple prayer made it all happen.

A few days later, I took Rob and Nancy's brother back up to Guerneville so they could go in by boat and check out the damage. They found that the floodwaters had stopped just below a framed prayer hanging on the entry wall of the house. That prayer had been a gift from Harriet's aunt in Fayetteville, North Carolina.

They returned to their home a week after the floods had driven them out. Two days later we got another call. Only this call was a blessing, as we were introduced to Christian Daniel Dawson Smith —7 pounds, 11 ounces.

Just His will.

Coincidence is one of God's ways of remaining anonymous.
—Doris Lessing

Fire "Captain Bob" Smith is a recognized expert and speaker on stress, communication, and relationship skills. He is the author of *Fire Up Your Communication Skills* (Code 3 Publications, 1997). www.eatstress.com

46

Unusual Roads

by Joanne Wallace

My grandson, Elijah, was adopted from Ethiopia and came to the United States when he was 10 years old. A couple of years before his arrival in this country, he was walking down a road in Ethiopia when he came alongside a truck being loaded with heavy crates. At that very moment, the crane lifting the cargo suddenly lost its load. Before Elijah could move out of the way, the crates crashed down upon him.

The force of the impact threw Elijah face down onto the ground as the cargo landed on his back and legs. Both his legs were broken, with the left leg suffering a very bad compound fracture.

Unable to afford medical treatment, Elijah's birth father took his severely wounded son home. There Elijah's stepmother (his birth mother had died 2 years before) and his two younger sisters tried to take care of him. Unfortunately, within a few days the left leg became infected with gangrene. Ten days after the accident, Elijah was near death. His father took him to a hospital several hours away in Addis Ababa, the capital of Ethiopia.

Doctors immediately decided to amputate the infected leg. It was an excruciating decision, but the only one that would save the boy's life. Even after the amputation, Elijah was still not out of danger; the next 2 weeks were critical for his survival.

As the doctors worked to save Elijah's life, his father worried about how he would pay the mounting medical costs, and how he would take care of Elijah after his recovery. With scant resources to feed his family, and little hope for disabled people in Ethiopia, Elijah's father was faced with the knowledge of a bleak future for his son. Knowing that Elijah could only be helped if he stayed at the hospital with trained medical personnel and ongoing treatment, his father made a heart-rendering decision. He abandoned Elijah at the hospital and never came back.

For the next year-and-a-half, Elijah lived at the Black Lion Hospital in Addis Ababa. There he slowly regained his health, and even attended school for the first time. Although he never saw his birth family again, Elijah became close to some of the hospital workers. They loved and cared for him along with other children who had been similarly abandoned there.

During this time my daughter, Deanna, was working with an adoption agency, helping to find homes for Ethiopian children. One day a small packet arrived on her desk at work. Inside there were photographs of Ethiopian children needing homes; the packet contained two photographs of Elijah.

Just one look at Elijah's photographs and my daughter immediately fell in love with his beautiful face, intelligent eyes, and courageous smile. In that instant, God spoke to Deanna's heart. Out loud she said to her co-worker, "This one is *mine!*"

Her words were not lightly spoken. A few months later, she flew to Ethiopia and brought Elijah home as her new son and eighth child.

When he was abandoned at the hospital, I'm sure that there was no way that Elijah could have foreseen that his life would someday have joy again. It probably never occurred to him that his life could take such unusual roads, roads that would eventually lead him to a new family on the other side of the world.

But God *did* foresee it. In His far-reaching plans, even the worst of events and circumstances can be transformed into joy.

When I look at Elijah now, with his smiling eyes as he walks around with his new prosthetic leg, I am reminded of the story of Joseph in the Bible. Joseph's brothers sold him into slavery and meant to cause him great harm. God, however, had another plan, and used Joseph's tragic circumstances to bring about great good for Joseph, his family, and an entire kingdom. (Read this story in Genesis 37, and 39-45).

Reflecting on Joseph and my grandson, I am reminded that God can transform my own difficult circumstances in mighty ways. It encourages me that God can take seemingly tragic events and make something beautiful out of them.

How about you? Are you struggling with your own version of tragic circumstances? Does it seem to you that God will never be able to make anything new or wonderful out of them? Take hope in Elijah's and Joseph's stories. Take hope as you consider *your* story. Understand that God can transform tragedy into great joy.

And we know that all things work together for good to them that love God, and to them who are called according to his purpose.

—Romans 8:28

Reprinted from the book, *As Refreshing as Snow in the Hot Summertime: Stories to Energize Your Faith, Lighten Your Spirit, and Deepen Your Hope* by Joanne Wallace (Wallace, 1998). It is used here with her kind permission. Joanne, the author of nine books, is a speaker for Christian conferences, and holds the designation CPAE (Council of Peers Award of Excellence) from the National Speakers Association. Contact: 1825 SW Coast Avenue, Lincoln City, OR 97367. (541) 994-3550.

47

A Solemn Salute

by "Peanut" Adams

The train station in Sparta, Wisconsin was a sad place that spring morning of 1943. Training was over, so soldiers who had their families still with them took their wives and children to the station to send them home. After the Louisiana Maneuvers, then cold weather training in Wisconsin, the Second Infantry Division finally had their orders to Europe. These soldiers would be boarding troop ships headed for Ireland and final staging. Their ultimate goal: Join with others to defeat the rascal Hitler on his own soil.

Paw Paw carried my great-aunt Kay onto the train while my great-grandmother Nana took her seat. As my great-grandfather gently placed his infant daughter into the arms of his wife, I can only imagine the emotion that came over them. Before he kissed them good-bye, Paw Paw removed a tiny bow from Kay's hair and placed it in his wallet.

What happened next is so vivid in Nana's memory. While most of the other soldiers left the station after putting their families aboard, Paw Paw remained on the platform as the train pulled away. She watched as he removed his cap and held it over his heart. It was a solemn salute, I'm sure; perhaps it was even a gesture of resolve that, someday, they would be together again. Nana says Paw Paw held that salute until he, the platform, and the station were out of sight.

History favored this story and this family. Paw Paw drove a truck onto Omaha Beach during the invasion of Normandy. Ultimately, he drove that truck right into Germany. They were victorious, but at a cost. Paw Paw came home to his family; Nana's brother didn't.

I look forward to a full and happy life every bit as good as what Paw Paw and Nana have enjoyed for many years. But I also know there will be times of difficulty along the way. During those times, I will hold to faith and family, just as Paw Paw has held onto that little piece of ribbon for almost 60 years. And I know that, if the time ever comes for me to exercise the courage of my great-grandparents, I'll do just fine.

After all, it's in the blood.

"Peanut" was the nickname for the unborn child of Brian and Katie Adams of Clear Lake, Texas. This story was written by grandpa-to-be, Jim Sutton. Jim is a Vietnam veteran, and the publisher of this book. Jim's wife, Bobbie, is the youngest daughter of Paw Paw and Nana (Robert and Margaret Richardson of Pleasanton, Texas).

Editor's Note: "Peanut" is now Jake Lewis Adams. He was born just before this book went to press.

48

Vecmam's Cross

by Vilis Ozols

As a professional speaker, I was doing a presentation last year in St. Catharine's, Ontario (near Niagara Falls). Because I was speaking in the very town where my grandmother lives, I arranged to have dinner with her the night before my presentation.

To do the evening justice, and to properly set the stage, I must give you a description of my grandmother, my "Vecmam," as she is called in Latvian. "Vec" means old and "mam" means mother in Latvian; hence, "Vecman," or "old mother."

My Vecmam (pronounced "vets-mum") is 88 years old. She came to Canada from the old country, Latvia, a small nation in northeastern Europe, right across the Baltic Sea from Sweden and Finland. She owned a vineyard and grew grapes commercially all her life. My Vecmam has worked the earth, and will probably have perpetual earth stains under her fingernails.

She is also very stern, opinionated, outspoken, and a dominating woman—the matriarch of our family. What she says, goes; no room for argument. Her "take charge" manner is made even more difficult by her advancing years and a progressive loss of hearing. Of course, she stubbornly refuses to wear her hearing aid.

I'm sure you can't completely picture my Vecmam from these few words, but she fits the stereotype of the "ethnic" grandmother. As much as I love her, I must admit that, after almost 2 hours into our evening together, I was reaching for my excuses—trying to find a way to make my exit. Perhaps you've been in the same situation; a duty visit, maybe even a mercy stopover. At some point you meet your responsibility; then it's okay to leave. Enough is just that — enough.

In the process of saying my goodbyes, I had just about made it out the door. That's when this 88-year-old woman grabbed my biceps in her gnarled hands, and held on with a vice-like grip.

Standing there in the entryway to her home she told me a story that would have a profound effect on my life. "Little Vili," she said, looking up at me, "when we were leaving the old country we were caught between the advancing Russian army and the retreating Nazis. Evil was everywhere!"

Her voice now took on a quiet, but emphatic, sing-song quality. I could tell she had something very important to tell me. As she spoke, her mind journeyed back to the past as she relived the experience.

"It was a little town in Germany...Breslau. We were surrounded. I'll never forget."

She paused for a moment, remembering, and then continued, "My husband ... ," her face beaming with his memory, "your grandfather, Vilis Ozols ... that's where you got your name!" She said it with great excitement, remembering that I was his namesake.

I almost said something sarcastic. I *knew* the source of my name. Let's face it; you don't go through life in today's modern America with a name like "Vilis Ozols" and not know how you got labeled with such a mouthful! But in that instant her tone changed to a quiet, more troubled monotone as she went on with her story. I was glad I had kept silent.

"That night ... he died ... your grandfather. And we still had to escape; we had no choice if we were to survive. I made arrangements to have him buried."

She reflected for a moment, then continued in the same, soft monotone. "I don't even know where he's buried." Her voice nearly cracked as she again dealt with the torment of a decision made over 50 years ago.

"And we *did* escape. The only thing I could salvage was the ring from his finger," she said with sad finality. The memory was obviously still quite painful.

"Later, in this new country," she continued, with pride in her voice, "I took his wedding band and my wedding band, and had them melted down and made into a cross. Since then, I have worn that cross every day of my life."

My Vecmam reached under her flannel bathrobe and removed a gold chain holding a substantial gold cross. She cradled the cross in her arthritic fingers, then held it out in front of her with loving reverence for the life and memories it represented.

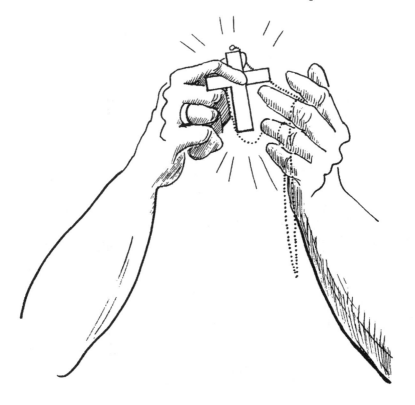

"Little Vili," she said, looking at the cross, and then to me, "I don't know when I will ever see you again. I want you to have this." She removed the cross and handed it to me.

I can't begin to describe the flood of emotions that ran through my mind. I know we cried together for a long time.

The cross was heavy in my hand, its value to me beyond price. I started to put it in a safe place —my wallet. Vecmam caught my wrist, her head shaking, "No!"

"You must wear this," she said, as she stretched to reverently place it around my neck. I don't exactly know how to describe my feelings at that moment, but I experienced something profoundly human, yet profoundly spiritual, at the same time. In that instant, I was reminded of how often we focus on the little things in our lives while losing sight of the truly important things—things like our family, our spirit, our legacy, and our humanity.

A few weeks later, I was visiting with my father, Vecmam's son. He shared with me what he remembered of that terrible experience. He was only 8 years old when he, his mother, and an older brother and sister were caught between enemy forces. He remembered another item belonging to Vilis Ozols that had been salvaged. Grandfather, a former detective in the Riga Police, had a pistol. My father, the youngest child, was given the responsibility of carrying and concealing that pistol. Had he been searched, and the pistol discovered, it could have meant incarceration or even death at the hands of the Nazis.

My father also shared a remarkable epilogue to the story of their escape. In the midnight hours following my grandfather's death, my Vecmam did something truly remarkable and heroic. With subzero temperatures threatening her family with death by exposure, with the death of her beloved Vili fresh on her mind, and with her arms wrapped around her three children, she brazenly confronted a group of Nazi soldiers who were guarding an abandoned factory. She actually shamed those soldiers into allowing her family and many other refugees to go inside the factory, taking shelter from the brutal elements outside.

Vecmam saved them all. My father said that he had never been more proud of his mother than at that moment. He added, paraphrasing the immortal words of Sir Winston Churchill: "It was her finest hour."

I now carry the weight of Vecmam's cross around my neck. It serves as a constant reminder to me of that which is truly important in life. I am also reminded of a beautiful phrase offered by Dr. Steven Covey:

We are not human beings having a spiritual experience; we are spiritual beings having a human experience.

Vilis Ozols lives in Golden, Colorado, with his wife, Andra, and his two sons. He is the president and founder of The Ozols Business Group, providing leadership training, motivational speaking, and business consulting. (800) 353-1030. www.ozols.com

49

Thunderstorm

by Miriam Burroughs Hall

It was a stormy summer afternoon in 1984. Vanessa, my 5-year-old granddaughter, was spending the day with me. The wind was howling and blowing; the thunder was clapping and cracking. A storm like this can be particularly harsh where we live—right on the top of a knoll that just seems to attract  thunderbolts. (It is so bad and so dangerous that our home and other buildings on the property are equipped with lightning rods.)

Vanessa had always been frightened by thunderstorms; this time was no exception. She was scared—even more afraid than usual. She was without her mother and father, and she wasn't even in her own home. We were alone.

As the storm developed, it was obvious that Vanessa was really frightened. I needed to try to calm her fears. I began to speak to her in a quiet way. I told Vanessa that God was always with us, even in thunderstorms. Together we would just ask him to take care of us and keep us safe. We would be all right.

We found a quiet place and talked to God. I moved the rocking chair from the family room to a safer place in the hallway (where there were no windows). I sat in the chair with Vanessa on my lap; I held her close in my arms. We rocked right through the storm. I sang songs very softly and hummed lullabies. Vanessa cuddled closely and stayed very still.

We remained that way, each holding the other, until the storm subsided. I put the chair back in its place after the storm had passed, then we returned to our normal sharing and visiting.

I never mentioned that thunderstorm incident again. However, one day, many years later, when Vanessa was 17, we were at my house talking about "life and things." Vanessa said to me: "Grandmother, do you remember how I used to be so afraid of storms when I was small? Well, I have never been afraid of a storm since that day we sat in the hallway and rocked."

Vanessa mentioned this lack of fear to me just a short time before she lost her young life in a tragic automobile accident. I am comforted by the thought of Vanessa — cuddled up in God's rocking chair, being consoled by the Author of Life.

Miriam B. Hall is a mother of five, grandmother of eight, and great-grandmother of six. In 1979, she was voted Mother-of-the-Year by the Home Demonstrations Club of Durham, North Carolina.

50

Braveheart

by Dottie Walters

When my children were young, they would come crying to me, as most children do, with skinned knees and other real or imagined hurts. I would put my arms around them and tell them, "We must find the 'still' together." The 'still' is a special place of peace and quiet.

"To do this," I would tell them, "take your right hand, put it under your left wrist, and gently place your fingers halfway across your arm—just above your left hand." They became so busy following my instructions the crying stopped. They began listening for what I would say next. I would say, "We have Scottish blood. Listen!"

I sang them the lilting words my Scottish grandpa used to sing to me:

I hear the bagpipes coming!
I hear the drummers drumming.
Braveheart, my heart's drum, drumming.
Scotland the Brave!"

Then I would say, "You see, your Scot's drums are *always* with you. Just as soon as you feel the beat of your drum be still—and think. Think about this question: 'What is the good thing, the best thing to do to solve my problem?'" I would continue, "you will always have the ability to think of the right thing to do in any emergency. Your Scot's Braveheart will give you the answer."

But that was a long time ago, and that good Scottish advice had faded with time. I was troubled. My husband had two strokes. I was trying to do his job and mine in our business, and I was making many trips to the hospital each day. I was stumbling. I felt lost.

One day, at the height of my difficulties, I needed to leave a message for my grandson Michael. He had a small, heavy-rock band. One of their recordings, loud and screaming, was the greeting on his answering machine. I hated to call his number because I really didn't like that sound; I didn't want to let him know just how awful I thought it was. Sometimes I wondered if he ever even remembered the sweet Scottish songs I used to sing to him.

My heart was truly heavy as I dialed his number. I braced myself for that blast of heavy sound. The phone rang. The answering machine sounded off, and I almost dropped the phone. My grandson had changed the recording. Playing in my ear were the welcome sounds of a real Scot's bagpipe band, skirling and swirling, beating out that wonderful tune, "Scotland the Brave."

Michael was telling me something. I got his message—loud and clear: "Braveheart, Nani. Braveheart."

Dottie Walters, *Certified Speaking Professional*, is president of Walters International Speakers Bureau. She is the publisher of "Sharing Ideas Magazine for Speakers and Authors." www.walters-intl.com

51

A Best Friend

by Marcia Riley-Elliott

By age 12, Marcia began to realize that she was living an abnormal and difficult childhood. Her stepfather was physically abusive toward her, and her mother was a victim of spousal abuse. With five children and no college education, Marcia's mom seemed trapped and bound to an unhappy marriage because she was financially dependent on her husband.

Many nights the police came to their house to stop the fighting. They usually took him for a ride to allow time for cooling off. Whenever it was Marcia who had called the police, she would tremble, fearful of his return and the retaliation he would inflict on her for calling. But she couldn't just stand helplessly by and watch her mother being beaten, even if it meant that she would be next.

She ran away from home several times, usually after a beating from her stepfather. Every time Marcia ran away, she headed straight for her granddaddy's house across the field. It was the one haven in her troubled life. But she was always forced to return home when her mother came to get her.

A warm welcome always greeted Marcia at her granddaddy's house. She felt special there. Even though her grandparents lived in a tin-roofed house with an outdoor toilet, a pot-bellied wood-burning stove, and only one water faucet on the back porch, it was the one place where she found real peace and was not threatened by physical violence. There she saw a positive male role model.

One day her stepfather had beaten Marcia so severely that she refused to change clothes for a P.E. class. She was defiant. She was not about to take off her clothes to put on gym attire; unusual behavior for an honor student. She was taken to the counselor's office.

This office visit changed her life. For the first time she cried out her story, showed the welts on her back, expressed her embarrassment of the other girls seeing those bruises, and asked for help. After hearing her story and seeing the evidence of the beatings, the counselor drove Marcia to a judge's office and told her not to leave until he saw the marks on her back. The counselor assured her that, once the judge knew what had been happening, she would never have to live with her stepfather again.

The judge talked with Marcia, had someone take photographs of her back, then sent her home. Later that week he met with Marcia and her mother and stepfather in his chambers.

Even though her mother attempted to defend the stepfather's actions (probably out of fear), telling the judge that Marcia was, "... the ruination of my life ... a bad seed," the judge explained that no one should be beaten like that. Then he said something that brought a smile to Marcia's face. He told her mother that, if

Marcia ran away from home again, she would not be forced to return.

From that day on, Marcia lived with her granddaddy and his second wife. She often thought of her three sisters and brother left behind. Since she was the only stepchild, however, she didn't think her stepfather would inflict those beatings on the other children.

At long last, Marcia was enjoying a loving and supportive family environment. She knew that her granddaddy never finished elementary school, and could not read or write, but he constantly advised her, "Get all the education you can so you can take care of yourself in life and not have to live with someone just because you need money."

Like his father before him, her granddaddy worked as an orange picker and was in charge of a crew. To reinforce his point about education, he would take Marcia to work with him in the orange groves. When she couldn't fill even one crate in a day, he would laughingly remind her that she needed to be educated and work with her mind. "Marcia," he said, "you'll starve if you have to do *outside* work."

Marcia grew in wisdom from the frequent front porch talks with her granddaddy. She admired his kind heart and sense of fairness. She saw him as her rescuer and best friend. Marcia wanted to make him proud of her.

During these talks, he stressed the importance of an education and in choosing a good mate. He frequently cooked the meals. He helped clean the house and her step-grandmother helped in the yard. They were a team, and, at the end of the week they would put their money together to pay the family bills. He taught her that, in relationships, whoever had the best knowledge should make the decision. Just because a man might be the head of the household does not mean he should make, or could make, all the decisions.

Granddaddy taught Marcia to always respect and care about people, and to be willing to share information that could help others. He cautioned her to spend her time with successful people, not losers. Even though he experienced racial discrimination, he insisted that there are good and bad White folks just as there are good and bad Black folks. And Marcia's granddaddy constantly told her that her mother loved her, but that she had been powerless to protect her from her stepfather's rage.

Marcia knew how long and hard her granddaddy worked in the dusty orange groves, so she was always eager to show him her love and concern. On weekends she loved to give him a foot massage or pull a hair bump, anything to show just how much she appreciated living there.

She went grocery shopping with her grandparents; they would call a cab or pay a neighbor to take them to the store. Marcia wondered how her grandparents, who couldn't read, purchased certain food. She learned that they studied the photos of the food items on the containers, or they would look at the product through the packaging. Marcia remembered how she beamed when she came out of the store on that first trip; she now knew their clever shopping secret. She thought, "Wow! They have no formal education, but my grandparents are really smart people."

Marcia worked too. Her first job was that of a dishwasher at a country club. Her granddaddy encouraged her to never be ashamed of honest work.

When it rained, there was no work in the orange grove. Still, her granddaddy refused to accept government food assistance. He always said that there were people who couldn't work, and they had more need for the help. So, Marcia learned to enjoy meatless meals, a small price to pay for the happy home life she was now enjoying.

She knew her granddaddy's story, and treasured it. He was born in 1911, and was raised with five brothers and two sisters on the Kitchen's Mill plantation in Aiken, South Carolina. He had to quit school to work on the farm. When his father went to DeLand, Florida, to work in citrus groves, Marcia's granddaddy and his brothers worked and saved money so that the family could reunite. Her granddaddy was the more vocal one, stressing that it was important for his mother and father to be together. So, after years of saving their hard-earned money, the whole family was moved to Florida.

Marcia graduated from high school with honors and went on to college, where she earned her bachelor's degree. She taught high school for several years, then got married. She was surprised to discover that, within the first year of marriage, her husband had an affair. When she confronted him with the facts, he beat her so badly that she went to the hospital. Recalling her childhood experiences and her granddaddy's wise guidance, Marcia divorced him.

With her granddaddy's encouragement, and a number of scholarships, Marcia completed her graduate studies. By age 28, she had earned her doctorate in education from Florida State University. She wanted her best friend to be proud of her academic achievements.

He was.

Marcia became an Assistant Professor at Western Kentucky University, where she taught vocational teacher education. Later, she moved to Knoxville and worked at the University of Tennessee, where she intended to eventually start her own business.

It was during her years in Knoxville that Marcia was finally able to resolve her issues with her mother. After a weekend in Life Training Therapy, Marcia called her mom and said, "I forgive you for my childhood experiences, and I forgive myself for being so bitter toward you for all these years. I now realize you did the best you could do at the time, and I have let go of the pain."

That one call enabled Marcia and her mother to renew their relationship and establish a bond.

When her granddaddy passed on in 1990, it was an extremely difficult time for Marcia. He had been her substitute father, mentor, role model, and best friend. During the funeral she never shed a tear, and even refused to view the casket. She grieved in her own way—in silence.

After returning to her work in Tennessee (and after several months of silent tears), Marcia reasoned that there were other youngsters who had experienced difficult childhoods. She had never shared a word about her childhood pain, but after some deep reflection about it, Marcia decided to put aside her shame and talk to student groups. She wanted to encourage them, and show them that, regardless of their home environment, there is hope for a better live.

She began speaking at schools and non-profit organizations that focused on youth. Whenever a student would question if she *really* knew what it was like to be severely beaten, Marcia would proudly show the scars of her childhood. She wanted to make a difference in their lives, and she wanted her *best* friend to be proud of the investment he had made in her.

Somewhere out there in the world beyond, Marcia felt he was proud!

Marcia Riley-Elliott, PhD, is the mother of two teens and owner of EA Incorporated, a consulting firm that provides training, editing, writing and speaking services to corporate, government and academic clients.

5 2

A Gift of Love

by David Crary

Daniel Huffman watches on the sidelines of a high school football field as movie stars film a scene in "The Daniel Huffman Story."

"It's way too strange," the Florida State student says.

Not many 20-year-olds have movies made about them. But not many did what Huffman did—he gave up his football career by donating a kidney to his grandmother.

Huffman's act of love occurred the summer before his senior year at high school in Rossville, Illinois, the small town where his grandparents raised him following his parents' divorce. His grandmother, Shirlee, badly needed a kidney transplant. There were fears she might die while waiting for a suitable donated kidney.

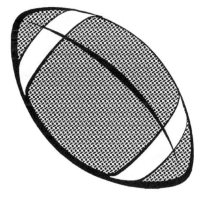

Daniel decided to make the donation himself, even though losing one of his kidneys meant he would have to give up football and other contact sports forever. He was a starting defensive tackle on the Rossville team and had to shelve plans to play in college.

Since then, there's been a lot of good news for Huffman. His grandmother is now healthy, and he received a full scholarship to Florida State as a student trainer with the football team. That deal came thanks to Seminoles coach Bobby Bowden, who first heard Huffman's story when each of them was honored at a football awards ceremony.

Huffman is now the subject of a movie: "A Gift of Love: The Daniel Huffman Story." Producer Daniel Paulson said, "Everybody is worried these days about young people and drugs and sex and violence, and President Clinton says Hollywood is not doing its part. This is a movie that really goes against that grain—it's a true profile in courage." Huffman is played by Elden Henson (one of the stars of "The Mighty Ducks"); his grandmother is played by Debbie Reynolds, and Bowden plays himself.

"My grandma was just completely thrilled," Huffman said.

"Here's a kid—he probably had a future in football, and he gave up his kidney for his grandmother," Bowden said. "You don't see young people doing things like that—I just never heard of anything more valiant."

Huffman hopes the movie will move those who see it. "I hope it will make people think more about organ donation," he said. "They'll become more educated about it and sign organ donor cards." He insists that his act was not as heroic as his admirers contend.

"If you love someone and you can help them—anyway you can—you're going to do it."

This Associated Press feature appeared in newspapers on July 8, 1999 under the byline of David Crary. It is reprinted here with permission (with some editing to this format).

53

Never Give Up
by Zig Ziglar

I had the privilege of baptizing Amanda Gail Stevens, my granddaughter whom I have always called "Sunshine," when she was 12 years old. Over the years she departed from her faith, dropped out of church, and got involved in drugs and many of the things drugs lead to.

In the latter part of 1997, tired, frustrated, and full of despair over the direction her life had taken, Amanda started praying, asking God to give her a love for Him. He did—big-time! Those who know her well, agree they have never seen such a radical transformation in *anyone*. Virtually every facet of her life changed completely. Today she is highly energetic and bubbles with excitement and enthusiasm. She goes out of her way to accommodate others and she is incredibly grateful for, and appreciative of, anything anyone does for her. She truly is an absolute delight to be around.

Amanda registered to take classes at the Lindale, Texas, base of *Youth With a Mission*, a training school for missionaries. They start with 3 months of intensive training, then go on a short mission trip to see if they are suited to become missionaries and if they truly feel God's call to the mission field. Her first trip was to Mongolia, and, despite all the hardships and difficulties she encountered, she loved it. Today she's on another mission, traveling by van with several other YWAM students, sharing the good news about her Savior in the inner cities of the Southwest and the Northwest.

This story, however, carries two significant messages. I was saved on July 4, 1972, largely because of the efforts of an elderly African-American lady who spent the weekend in our home. After I invited Christ to be my Lord and Savior, I got real excited about the significant changes that took place in my life—I had greater peace of mind and increased love for my wife, children, friends, associates, and the list goes on. The effectiveness of my presentations increased dramatically when I began using and teaching biblical principles in my material.

At the time Amanda began her personal relationship with Christ, I had been teaching Sunday school for 15 years. I was faithful in my Bible reading, though there were days when I did miss reading it, and other days when I "dutifully" read a chapter or two. But when I saw how excited Sunshine was about Jesus, I started asking God to give me the same love and excitement for Him and His message. I also made an unbreakable, irreversible, irrevocable commitment that, come what may, I would study my Bible every day. Since that date in December of 1998, I have faithfully done that.

The most beautiful part of the story as far as my personal benefits are concerned, however, is how God is showing me new things—which have been in His Book all of the time! It's amazing, but when you get closer to the Author, His Word means infinitely more to you.

First message: Bread cast upon the waters comes back many times buttered and toasted to a delicious golden brown. Because I was reasonably active in Sunshine's life, especially when she was a baby and toddler, and to a fairly large degree throughout her childhood, I had no idea that, when she became a beautiful young adult, she would be the instrument God would use to draw me closer to Him. So, parents and grandparents, it's important what you teach your children and grandchildren. Who knows, maybe the day will come when they will teach *you* even more!

Second message: You should never give up on your children or grandchildren. Keep faith in them. Continue to encourage and pray for them. If they have a stabilizing influence and constant assurance that they are loved and that you do care, there is no telling what can happen down the road. We need to remember for our own lives, and for those we love, that failure is an event and not a person—that yesterday ended last night and today is a brand new day. People can change, and change radically. If you don't believe me, ask Sunshine. She'll tell you. But she will also tell you that God is the agent of change in the person of Jesus Christ.

Zig Ziglar, CPAE, is the chairman of the Dallas-based Zig Ziglar Corporation. Zig, a member of the Speakers' Hall of Fame, is recognized by many to be the benchmark of professional speaking.

54

Holding the Flag for America

by Al McCree

I retired from the United States Air Force in 1989 after a successful 20-year career as a fighter pilot, instructor pilot, and maintenance commander. This career included three great overseas tours. We had lots of good friends and memories, but it was time for a change. We moved to Nashville so I could pursue a musical dream.

On reflection, the move has been a good one. The family was happy; I founded a successful record company; I did some professional speaking and performing, and I made some money.

On Jan 17, 1991, I gave a luncheon speech on leadership to the Tennessee Trucking Association. That evening I went to the Wednesday night church dinner at the Brentwood United Methodist Church, just like a lot of people do on Wednesday nights. At about 6:30 that evening, the assistant minister came in and asked for quiet, then asked for prayer. He announced that we were at war. It was the beginning of Desert Storm.

I was instantly transformed to my past military life; I had a lot of friends still on active duty. I had trained many of the pilots who flew in the desert. Colonel Dave Eberle was one of the first pilot shot down; we had flown together in San Antonio, Texas.

That night my body was in Tennessee, but my heart was in the desert.

Out of that experience I wrote a song. The song, however, is about more than Desert Storm. It is dedicated to anyone who has ever worn the uniform of the United States or to anyone who has ever had a relative, or a close friend who wore, or wears, the uniform of our country.

If you go to a football game or a parade, the color guard is almost always military. That's because the military is *Holding the Flag for America*. This song is for those who are serving. It is for those who served, and it is for those who had husband and wives, brothers and sisters, and sons and daughters who were and are *Holding the Flag for America*.

And, because this book is about grandparents, I offer a special tribute to the grandfathers and grandmothers who proudly served and supported our flag and all it represents. May we always cherish it, and proudly hold it high.

I remember crying the night that Saigon fell.

I remember Vietnam, I remember well

My roommate who died there

and friends in prison cells,

Holding the flag for America.

My father told me stories
of his days in World War II.
MacArthur in New Guinea,
And the things they had to do.
He didn't see his baby girl
Till after she was two.
He was holding the flag for America.

The world is always changing.
Tyrants rise and fall.
In Moscow they have McDonald's now,
And in Berlin they tore down the wall.
And I'd like to think it was because
A few of us stood tall,
Holding the flag for America.

'Twas a storm out in the Middle East
Underneath the desert sun.
The diplomats, they failed,
So we had to use the gun.

And all our sons and daughters
Did what must be done,
Holding the flag for America.

And as we go about our lives,

And as we stop and pray,

We must preserve the way of life

That brought us here today.

And each and every one of us

In our own special way

Is holding the flag for America.

And each and every one of us

In our own special way

Is holding the flag for America.

Holding the flag;

We are holding the flag;

We are holding the flag for America.

"Holding the Flag for America" is by Al McCree (© 1992). Today Al is a professional speaker and founder of Altissimo! Records, the ultimate source for America's greatest military bands, orchestras, and ensembles.

55

Faith, Commitment, and a New Grandchild

by Naomi Rhode

My mother was with me when I received my eternal heritage. On that most significant and memorable day, I committed my life to Christ. From that point on, my faith and family, and the legacy they represent, have been the central part of everything that is me. I am so blessed—and so grateful.

My husband Jim and I have been blessed with the birth of five grandsons over the last 3 years. While anticipating the birth of our fifth (Beth and Curt's third son) I promised Beth that I would be with her in the delivery room if at all possible—just as I had tried to do as each new grandchild was born.

A few days before the baby was due, I was scheduled to speak to an audience of about 500 at a seminar in Eugene, Oregon. The seminar had been planned for over a year; I needed to meet that obligation. I needed to be there. The night before I was to speak, Beth informed me she might be delivering early. I assured her I would hurry to her in California just as soon as I had finished speaking.

That morning as I spoke, I shared with the audience that a definition of a true professional was someone who does even better when they don't *feel* like doing it. I told them that, frankly, my heart was with Beth that day. At the same time, I assured them I would be at my very best because of my personal commitment to them.

As I came to the end of the first session, I told them a story I often tell about the first baby heart transplant at Loma Linda Hospital. A young couple in Michigan had a baby who was dying; they had agreed to donate the heart of their baby to a child at Loma Linda who desperately needed the transplant.

Jim and I happened to be visiting the hospital the day the baby was scheduled for surgery. While there, we caught the buzz of a rumor that the helicopter, carrying the needed heart, had arrived and was landing. The air was electrified; we were filled with anticipation and excitement.

A week after the surgery, I saw a photograph of the donor family in *Time* magazine. The magazine contained an interview in which the mother of the infant donor told how she had gone to say goodbye to her little boy. She told how she had rubbed his tiny arms and said, "Now you do a very good job."

And he did.

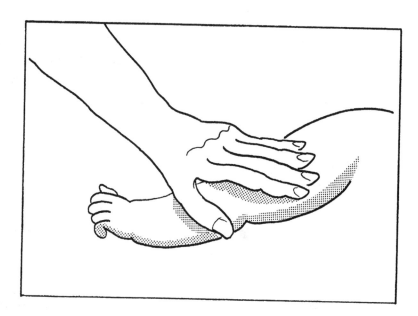

Each time I tell that story, I offer a challenge to the audience. I compare the very few days the donor child had lived and what he had given to the many more days we have lived, and continue to live. I suggest that, each day, we should look at ourselves in the mirror and ask if we have done well with the time we have been given. I closed that session with a poem; the audience burst into applause.

Suddenly the audience of 500 was not only clapping, but were gasping and even crying. Confused, I noticed they were pointing to the overhead projector screen just behind me. I turned around to read this message:

IT'S A BOY!

QUINLAN JEFFERY HAMANN

6 LBS. 5 OZ.

Score: Grandsons=5, Granddaughters=0

I wept and the audience wept. The applause continued. The tears and applause were meant to honor new life, new hope, new sharing. They honored one more child of God who will receive a lasting legacy of love. I promise.

God has given us eternal life, and this life is in His Son.
—I John 5:11

But as many as received Him, to them He gave the right to become children of God, even to those who believe in His name.
—John 1:12

Naomi Rhode, CSP, CPAE is a professional speaker from Phoenix, Arizona. She is a member of the *Speaker's Hall of Fame*, a recipient of the Cavett Award, and past president of the National Speakers Association. Naomi and Jim also own and operate Smart Practice, a national resource to the dental profession.

56

The Journey
by Vilis Ozols

Due to the remarkable abilities of our mother, it is difficult for me to say that my sister and I were raised in a low-income environment. Mother found a way to stretch and utilize every penny she earned while we were growing up. She was a single parent raising us on a secretary's salary, working overtime and "moonlighting," as she called it, taking on extra jobs, just to make ends meet. It was only after I started working and earning on my own that I realized how truly remarkable my mother was—how her work ethic helped make bare sufficiency seem almost opulent.

I was in my third year at the university when an extraordinary opportunity came my way. The offer came from my earliest true friend in life, Vivian, who was, at the time, employed in a Foreign Service position in the Far East. She had a round-trip airline ticket, a benefit of her Asian posting, but it needed to be used by the end of the year. She was not in a position to use the ticket, and her immediate family had also declined its use. When she offered this free "round-the-world" ticket to me, I gratefully accepted it without a second thought.

My real problem was finding the money I needed to make the trip. I had been barely able to put myself through school utilizing available assistance, working full-time at the university pub, and my mother's generous response to my "Dear Mom: I'm broke!" letters. My life at the university had become a blur. I was a full-time student, worked full-time in the evenings, and was a full-time varsity athlete. The trip would be a welcome break from my hectic school schedule. Besides, the timing was perfect; the semester was about to end.

I was full of excitement when I called my mom to tell her of this splendid travel possibility. The silence that followed was my first hint that my enthusiasm was not shared by the remarkable woman I call Mother. She understood all too clearly the reality of the financial demands of this "free" trip. She quickly enlightened me; I simply could not afford a trip of this magnitude. She mentioned hotel expenses, meals, and ground transportation. She also reminded me that the semester break was the time to work to pay the next semester's tuition.

My decision to proceed with the trip, in spite of the financial problems, caused a deep rift in my relationship with my mother. We had scraped and saved pennies for years to live the dream of my attending the university and completing a degree. It must have seemed to this extraordinary woman that I was throwing away my chance to succeed—all for a travel whim, a frivolous trip. We had many silent moments leading up to my departure.

The trip was everything I had hoped it would be, and more. I traveled around the world to England, Bahrain, Thailand, Hong Kong, China, Japan, and the United States—savoring experiences I would remember for a lifetime. On the third day of my stay in Hong Kong, I was offered a job. I stayed there for 6 months, modeling, acting, and bartending. The trip taught me so much about self-sufficiency, and it gave me self-confidence. I had truly become a citizen of the world. It was a growing-up experience that has impacted my life and personal development—even to this day.

When I finally arrived back home, the pursuit of graduation was delayed; I had to take another semester off to earn tuition. I had even given thought to not completing school at all. Meanwhile, the rift between my mother and me had not lessened; it had actually gotten worse. We were able to eventually work through it all, however, and I remember well her immense pride when I finally *did* graduate from the university.

My mother rightfully questioned my judgment and decisions during these learning occasions (as moms are known to do). Our differences usually centered on money and the way it should be spent. During those discussions, I always felt that my round-the-world trip was a wordless shadow that cast nothing but darkness on our relationship. Would she *ever* forget?

Well, many years later in Denver, at the birth of our first son, Aldis (a joyous, life-defining event for all of us), my mother welcomed her firstborn grandson in style. And Vivian, my trip benefactor of long ago, became his godmother.

Gifts were given in abundance during those early months. But one gift stands out as being very special because, in the giving, it united three generations and healed the rift between mother and son forever. My mother, in private, handed me an envelope. With a grandmother's wisdom she simply said, "You invest this money, and, when your son is old enough, you be absolutely sure that you use it for him to go on a trip—just like *you* did!"

Two years later, our second son, Talis, was born. He received the same gift from his grandmother, with the same mandate: "To go on a trip—just like you."

A picture is worth a thousand words. A journey is worth a thousand books.
—Chinese proverb

Don't let School interfere with your education.
—Mark Twain

Vilis Ozols lives in Golden, Colorado, with his wife, Andra, and his two sons. He is president and founder of The Ozols Business Group, providing leadership training, motivational speaking, and business consulting. (800) 353-1030. www.ozols.com

57

Water Works!

by Debbie Allen

My grandmother is an inspiration. She's an inspiration to me and to the many others she touches every day of her life. What a joy it is to have her in my life; she is one of the most incredible people I know. Her zest for life, her genuine enthusiasm, and her wonderful sense of humor touch everyone she meets.

In 1993, Bernadette Dault was certainly not the healthy and active person she is today. Her health was failing; high blood pressure and constant pain left her dependent on the support of a walker or a cane just to get around. She was bent over at the shoulders and could barely open her fingers because of crippling arthritis. Pain pills and a tremendous amount of sleep made it barely possible for her to cope with life day to day. She became frustrated when her doctors told her there was nothing else they could do for her condition. She became weaker, and very depressed.

Grandmother decided to try another doctor—one last hope. The new doctor suggested water aerobics.

"Oh, no!" she responded. "I don't go into water. I'm deathly afraid of being in a pool; the nearest I ever come to a body of water is a walk on the beach." Not only was she afraid of water, but she was also afraid of exercise. Exercise of any kind caused her so much pain.

Reluctantly, as a last and perhaps only hope for freedom from pain and discomfort, she decided to give water aerobics a try. As she sat on the steps of the swimming pool on that first day she was nervous, shaky, afraid, and hesitant to go into the water. But the physical therapist was able to persuade her to walk across the shallow end of the pool with the aid of her walker. She did it.

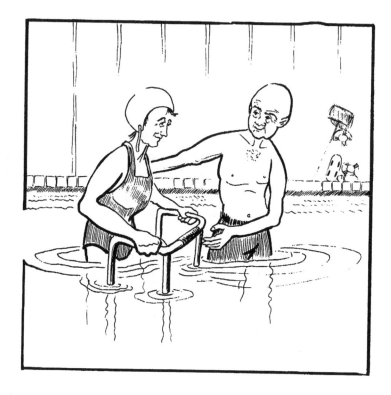

With each day she found the exercise a little easier. With the help of her first water aerobics instructor, a 90-year-old man, Grandmother gained confidence and stamina.

"I knew I couldn't give up," she told me. She was determined to stay with the program—no matter how difficult. "I didn't want to feel sick or be in pain any more," she shared.

She *did* stay with it. Before long my grandmother no longer needed the help of a therapist. She even joined a health club. There has been so much progress since those first few frightening days in the water.

Water works. It *really* works.

Grandmother is now free of that terrible arthritic pain, and she lives an active life. She is having the time of her life; as happy as she has ever been. Now a healthy 90-year-old, she teaches water aerobics at a retirement community where she lives. She encourages other seniors to get involved. Her social life has blossomed also. She serves on the Welcoming Committee, and just recently took up line dancing!

My grandmother; I'm her biggest fan.

Debbie Allen is an international professional speaker, consultant, and author specializing in business image and retail trade. www.DebbieAllen.com

58

Let the Candle Burn

by Linda Tobey

Every winter, during the season of darkness, I light candles to honor my grandmother. Whether lighting the Menorah for the Festival of Lights, Hanukkah, or just warming a room with a scented candle, I remember a long-ago moment—and a story.

When I was a teenager, years after the novelty of driedel games of childhood Hanukkah celebrations wore off, my mother and I would light the candles of the Menorah and sit together with the lights off, watching their flickering dance. Sometimes we were quiet; sometimes she told me stories.

One year she told me a story about my grandmother. In the 1930s, when my mother was about my age, they lived by the tracks. It was the time of the Great Depression. Hoboes would jump off the passing trains and knock on their back door. My grandmother would respond to every knock, giving food and coffee to those hoboes. In the tradition of the family, anyone in need was welcome at their home. Even though times were really hard, and *everyone* was poor, my grandmother always found something to share with others. Her mother had taught her to never let someone who was hungry pass by her gate.

For the weary traveler, an open home is a healing sight.

How was it that others knew this home would welcome them? The sign was a notch on the back gate and a candle burning in the window.

 For my mother, and for me, the lit Menorah belongs in our windows; its drops of light let passers-by know that this is a Jewish home, and that they are welcome here. Similarly, I want my life to be equally hospitable, welcoming the weary and the joyful alike.

Sitting in my darkened room, I watch a candle burn, and I observe the reflection in my window—a sign to the world. I remember my grandmother and my mother with a tender, poignant, candlelight of memory. I hope that who I am flickers light and hope into the darkness of our winters.

Let the candle burn from the window of my spirit to yours.

Linda Tobey is proud to hold a PhD in Human and Organizational Studies and certification as Master Coach. Her book, The *Integrity Moment*, is in process.

Part Three

Life's Moments

T hese stories show us how seemingly small events can become those special turning points in our lives that are always treasured—and never forgotten.

59

A Place for "Pop-Pop"

from "**Dear Abby**"

DEAR ABBY: This in response to the letter from "Appalled Cousin" concerning the grandfather who was disinvited from his granddaughter Lenore's wedding.

My newest daughter-in-law's wedding took place last June in La Jolla, California. Janene had planned for her "Pop-Pop" and grandmother to attend, but her grandmother passed away a couple of months before the event.

The day of the wedding, which was outdoors in a small public park by the beach, Pop-Pop was late in arriving. He's confined to a wheelchair and was running late. Janene simply said, "The wedding doesn't start until Pop-Pop gets here." We all waited, took photos of the wedding party, played with the grandchildren, and visited with relatives as the bride waited in the limousine for Pop-Pop to arrive. Because this was a public place, tourists on the sidewalk became curious and stopped to watch the festivities.

About an hour later, Pop-Pop arrived. The park was not wheelchair accessible, so he was carried by some strong young men, wheelchair and all, to his place of honor in the front.

Now Janene was ready. As if on cue, the sun broke through the gloomy overcast, the sky turned a vivid blue, the waves turned a brilliant white, and the wedding began. When the vows were exchanged there was cheering and applause from everyone, including the sidewalk gallery.

Pop-Pop was as radiant as Janene. He is in all the wedding pictures. Pop-Pop died recently, but he was thrilled to be in the wedding, and happy that his granddaughter had delayed it just for him.

I'm afraid Lenore just doesn't understand what a perfect wedding is all about.

I'm overjoyed to have such a terrific daughter-in-law come into my family. This girl is a real keeper. Pregnant with their first child, Janene graduated from college Summa Cum Laude this past June. The baby, like Pop-Pop, arrived late.

Some things are well worth waiting for.

—Paul Asgierson, proud father-in-law, Portland, Oregon

DEAR PAUL: Thank you for an upper of a letter. Your daughter-in-law, Janene, is indeed a prize.

<u>60</u>

Surrogate Grandparents

by Ernie Wendell

Not too long ago it was Grandparents' Day at the school my granddaughter attends. I received a special invitation to participate in the program. The opportunity to share before the assembled children and grandparents was a unique privilege. My granddaughter was especially pleased with my program presentation. She happily remarked, "You got more applause than anyone — even the principal."

After the auditorium program, all the eager grandparents were invited to visit the classroom(s) of their grandchildren. I proceeded to Mrs. Rebman's second grade classroom, where we enjoyed a delightful reading presentation by the students. Following the Thanksgiving (Pilgrim Story) rendition we were offered some light refreshments. Milk and cookie time is still one of the world's great treats; we should all do it more often.

While tightly squeezed into one of those small student-type chairs, munching on my cookies I noticed a gentleman and lady seated at a corner table with several of the 2nd-grade children. I recognized the man. Extracting myself from the chair, I walked across the room and addressed him.

"Are you Bill Friday?" I asked. (Bill Friday is easily recognized in North Carolina as the past chairman of the vast University of North Carolina system. He is also a TV personality.)

He looked up at me from a low, near the floor table, and with a warm, friendly smile responded, "Yes, I am."

"Do you have a grandchild in *this* class?"

"No," he answered. "Mrs. Friday and I are here to support the children who don't have a grandparent present." He continued, "I'm Mrs. Rebman's Uncle Bill."

"How neat!" I commented, as we shared a hearty handshake.

Several weeks later I was telling a fellow airline passenger (a lovely young lady from New York who worked on the TV program "Sesame Street") about that special "Grandparents' Day," and how much I enjoyed it. She surprised me when she told me that she had hated that particular day when she was a young girl in school.

"Why would you hate Grandparents' Day?"

"Because," she said, "I didn't have any grandparents, and I always felt left out."

In a flash of insight, I understood the void she must have experienced as a little girl. And, from that experience I concluded that any children who are without grandparents—for any reason—deserve to have someone (like Bill and Ida Friday) to stand in and change a moment of possible sadness into one of gladness.

Any volunteers out there? No child should be without a grandparent—especially on Grandparents' Day.

Ernie Wendell is the compiler of *GRAND-Stories*. Ernie is an inspirational speaker and seminar leader. He is the author of the book, *Stepping Stones to Success* (Milestone Publications, 1997).

61

Alexander the Great

by Lois Wyse

Alexander, who lives in California, came with his parents to visit Grandfather and Grandmother in New York.

One day he was in a taxi with his grandparents, and, when the cab stopped for a traffic light, a rag-tag woman approached. With a toothless smile, she put her hand out to the driver.

Grandmother just happened to have a dollar-bill in her hand. "Here," she called, as he unrolled the window and handed the woman the bill.

The old woman nodded her appreciation.

Alexander, who observed this without speaking, turned then to the old, unkempt woman and blew her a kiss.

The cab drove on.

"That all happened in a twinkling," Grandmother reported, "but can you imagine the last time anyone blew a kiss to that woman?"

And now Grandmother wonders to herself and to Grandfather, "What can a family do to help a boy grow up without losing that sweet spontaneity?"

Reprinted from the book, *You Wouldn't Believe What My Grandchild Did* by Lois Wyse (Simon and Schuster, 1995). Used with the kind permission of the author and publisher.

62

Christmas Dinner

by Sally White

"It's pneumonia."

The doctor shook his head as he folded up his stethoscope and put it away. Dr. Herbert had taken care of me since I was a baby, and he had seen me safely through more than my share of childhood diseases.

"I should put her in the hospital, but I can't do that to a 5-year-old on Christmas Eve—unless I really have to," he said, pulling out his prescription pad.

Perched at the edge of the couch where I was lying, he gave my parents a series of instructions, restrictions, and conditions that would allow me to stay home for Christmas. I didn't say much. The word "hospital" would have shut me up even if I hadn't been a naturally quiet child. A third-grader had told me a nasty rumor about Santa Claus. I wasn't sure I believed her, but I was sure that Santa Claus, if he did exist, would never find me in a hospital bed.

After the doctor left, my dad started shrugging on a coat and searching for his car keys, hoping he could find a pharmacy that was still open. "I guess I'd better call," my mom said, the worry of a sick child evident in her face and in her voice. "You and Steve should go on to Christmas dinner at J.J.'s tomorrow; you can bring us back a plate. But I should let them know to set two fewer places."

My heart sank even further. Christmas just wouldn't be Christmas without dinner at my beloved J.J.'s. He was my grandfather, my mom's dad. My grandmother, Sara, died 5 months before I was born. My parents moved in with J.J. and my aunt Helen, who was only 15 at the time. The arrival of his first grandchild was a welcome distraction from his grief.

J.J. would come home from work and immediately seek me out to play. My mom would scold him for taking me out of the playpen. She was fixing dinner, so she wanted me in the playpen, out of harm's way. So J.J., tall and lanky, simply folded himself in two and climbed in the playpen with me. The playpen, with its bowed bottom, would serve several other grandchildren in my wake. Even after we moved back into our own home and he remarried, we retained a special bond.

The Christmas when I was 3, he had asked my mother what I needed for Christmas. "A new winter coat," she responded. Both of them were practical people, so they decided he would wait until January's coat sales before actually making the purchase.

But suddenly on Christmas Eve it hit him. There would be nothing under the tree the next morning that said, "To Sally, from J.J." He decided a tricycle was the appropriate gift, and rushed out to buy one.

Of course the only tricycle still on the store shelves late on the afternoon of Christmas Eve was the super-duper deluxe model, complete with plastic streamers on the handlebars that blew back when you peddled as hard as you could. And, it had a bell that really worked!

Delighted with his purchase, J.J. once more folded himself in two, looped his legs over the handlebars, and rode the tricycle around his house to my aunt's chorus of giggles. But the giggling stopped when J.J. realized that he had bent the back axle under his weight. He spent Christmas Eve in his workshop banging it back into shape.

Between the fever and the nasty-tasting medicine, I don't remember much of that Christmas Eve or Christmas morning when I was 5. Santa had come during the night (I knew that girl Adele didn't know what she was talking about), but I had little energy or enthusiasm for presents. Even when Daddy carried me to the door to see the real grown-up vanity table Santa had left me on the porch, I couldn't muster much excitement. After all, this was a second-best, make-do kind of Christmas. I couldn't go to church on Christmas Eve. I loved the candles and the smell of incense in the high-ceilinged Episcopal Church my family had attended for generations. I had just joined the children's choir that year, and took great delight in mangling the Latin refrains. But not on this Christmas, not for me.

Not to mention, I felt lousy.

But Christmas soon took a turn for the better, thanks to one inventive grandfather who was determined to make it a festive, loving Christmas. I didn't know that the day before, when Mom called to cancel, J.J. had proposed a different plan.

"No, no, Emily," he had said to my mother. "You need a break and a good, hot meal. It'll do you good to come over here and see the relatives on Christmas. I'll tell you what I'll do. I will go ahead and make up a plate for Sally and me and come and sit with her while you come over here."

A little before midday he showed up at the front door, bearing two heaping plates of Christmas feast. He shooed the rest of the family out the door, reassuring my mom that everything would be fine: He could handle it, and he'd call if she were needed.

I was too weak to sit at the table, so he propped me up on the couch with extra pillows, and then snuggled a folding TV tray up close. He unwrapped the many layers of aluminum foil that were keeping our dinner warm in that pre-microwave era. My plate had an extra big helping of rice and gravy (my favorite), which he hoped would tempt my feeble appetite.

After I dutifully recited, "God is great; God is good; now we thank Him for our food," we picked up our forks to dig in. But even before I could take a bite, J.J. leaned over, and, with a conspiratorial wink, said, "Isn't this wonderful? We get to have Christmas dinner together, just the two of us." And, suddenly, it was no longer a make-do kind of Christmas. In my mind it was a grand feast, at which I was the honored guest. The day took on a special radiance.

And I discovered I was hungry!

Sally White is a trainer, writer, and consultant specializing in teambuilding, customer service, management development and communications. She is with Russell J. White International, a firm in South Carolina.

6 3

Grandma and the Train Ride

by James D. Sutton

For a number of years I was the only grandchild on my mother's side of the family. For that reason my grandmother and I shared a very special relationship. When you're the *only* one, you get lots of attention.

One of my favorite memories about my grandmother goes back to the time when I had spent most of the summer with her and my aunt's family in Minnesota. I was about nine at the time. After summer vacation, Grandma and I made the return trip to Tulsa, Oklahoma, by train. Those were the days when only the well-to-do could even think of traveling by air.

We were well prepared. Armed with a couple of sacks of books, games, and plenty of snack food, Grandma and I boarded the train and settled into our seats for the 2-day trip. I can still remember watching the scenery go by, occasionally drifting in and out of sleep to the rhythm of the clickity-clack of steel wheels on steel rails.

For those folks riding through the night in coach (instead of the much more expensive Pullman sleeper cars), the porter would make his way down the aisle renting pillows. We only needed one. Grandma, an experienced rail traveler, always carried a big, down pillow with her.

In the morning, the train made a stop (in St. Louis, as I recall), so Grandma treated me to a hearty breakfast in the station cafeteria. When we re-boarded and returned to our coach seats, we discovered that the porter had taken up *all* the pillows, including Grandma's! She insisted that the porter sort through the piles and piles of pillows until he found the one that belonged to her. He finally brought her *a* pillow, but it wasn't *the* pillow (something he heard about all the way to Tulsa).

Thinking back, I suppose traveling by train with my grandmother stands out in my mind because it was a special adventure that was shared just between the two of us. Through the years we did a lot of things together. Grandma even taught me how to embroider a little and to bake sugar cookies. (We decided once to triple the recipe, and had more cookies than we could find jars, cans, and boxes to put them in; but that's *another* story.)

I was home on leave from the U.S. Navy when my grandmother passed away in 1968. It was a few days before my scheduled departure for a 2-year hitch in Japan. She was very sick, but she knew I was there, that I was still home. To this very day I believe she picked her time to go.

I've heard of these things happening.

Dr. Jim Sutton, Certified Speaking Professional, is an educator and psychologist who trains child service professionals. He is also the publisher of *GRAND-Stories*. (800) 659-6628. www.DocSpeak.com

64

The Bathroom Door That Wouldn't Lock

by Marjorie Brody

Nana Maggie was my grandmother. Her head of silver hair topped off her full five feet of extended height. Her lovely blue eyes always shone out with a ready, warm welcome. She was very special, and I loved her.

Periodically she would come to visit with my children and me for the weekend. One of those wonderful visits occurred shortly after she had experienced some radical surgery. My daughters Julie and Amy, were 3 and 5 years old.

Nana Maggie planned to take a nice, relaxing bath. However, she immediately discovered that the bathroom door lock was broken; the door wouldn't lock. She was very concerned that the girls might come in while she was in the process of bathing. She didn't want them to be alarmed, frightened, or disturbed by the possible viewing of the effects of that recent surgery. She enlisted me to stand guard while she undressed and got into the tub.

Right after she got into the tub, my front doorbell rang. I told Nana I would be back in just a moment and hurried to answer the door.

I was occupied with the visitor for about 15 minutes, when I suddenly remembered the door that wouldn't lock. I rushed back up the stairs and entered the bathroom. Sure enough, Amy and Julie had found their way into the room. I found them both seated on the edge of the tub, busily chatting away with Nana.

They hadn't noticed any disfigurement. My little girls were excited and pleased just being with their great-grandmother. Their love took them past the outer part of Nana and right to her heart. They were drawn to the inner person, the *real* Nana. They didn't pay the least bit of attention to the outer stuff; they didn't even see it. It just wasn't important.

When it comes to demonstrating unconditional love, our children (and grandchildren) can sometimes be marvelous teachers.

Marjorie Brody, CSP, CMC, Star Maker. She is a professional speaker, workshop leader and author. She works with organizations to help their people shine.

<u>65</u>

Thanks for the Memory

by Fire "Captain Bob" Smith

Fred is a grandfather in his 70s and still an active pilot. He is also still making memories.

Every year, there is an air show in Hayward, California. At the last show, there were two World War II bombers on display, a B-17 and a B-24. They were on their way to a larger air show in Watsonville, California, scheduled for a couple of days later.

Early every morning, Fred was out walking around the B-24. He would walk for awhile and then stop and just stare off into the distant sky. He had flown B-24s over Europe during World War II. And, not only did he fly this particular type of aircraft, but, believe it or not, he had flown *this very plane.*

It was his old ship. The ex-bomber pilot was flooded with memories.

Just before the two planes were scheduled to depart for Watsonville, the old pilot's wife and grandson surprised Fred with an announcement. The grandson stood proudly in front of his grandfather and said, "Grandpa, you're going with them! Grandmother and I have made arrangements for you to fly to Watsonville in the B-24."

Relating the story later the grandson added, "It was the first and only time I ever saw my grandpa cry." It was a splendid opportunity for Fred to revisit some cherished memories and past experiences—a real-life sentimental journey.

Those two old war birds took off with Grandpa in his original B-24 pilot seat. They made a fly-by, and then flew out over the San Francisco Golden Gate Bridge on their way to Watsonville.

Another memory for Fred—and one for his grandson also.

Fire "Captain Bob" Smith is a recognized expert and speaker on stress, communication, and relationship skills. He is the author of *Fire Up Your Communication Skills* (Code 3 Publications, 1997). www.eatstress.com

66

It's Hard to Explain My Behavior

by Linda Weltner

My daughter called the other day before picking up Jessie.

"Don't rush," I said cheerfully. "We're lighting matches."

There was a moment's silence, then a thoughtful, "I'll be there soon."

My daughter and her husband are trying to civilize my 2-year-old granddaughter. They're teaching Jessie to brush her teeth, pick up her toys, and restrain her impulse to bite. They want her to keep her food on her plate, the pages in her books, and her shoes on her feet.

It's hard to parent a child these days, and my natural inclinations aren't making it any easier for Laura and Brian. They're often taken aback at my style of babysitting.

They retrieved a child who's covered her chin with lipstick, smeared her cheeks with rouge, and streaked her forehead with eye shadow. The one time Laura turned to me for an explanation, I looked like a clown myself. Jessie had spent a good half-hour decorating my face with the contents of my make-up bag.

When I took Jessie to feed the ducks at the golf course, a multitude of geese appeared, determined to get at our load of bread one way or another. With Jessie on my shoulders, I had to fight my way back to the car through a cackling horde of determined waterfowl. The first time, we were taken aback. Now it's our idea of great adventure.

During a big storm last fall, I took Jessie to a neighbor's porch to watch enormous waves pounding against the rocks below. Huddled against the door high above them, we were in no danger of getting swept away, but we did get drenched. By the time I got Jessie home to her mom, her diapers were wet from the *outside*.

I like to let Jessie's imagination run wild, although we gave up painting with food coloring after it got under her nails and ruined her clothing. We now mix acrylic paints in ice cube trays and paint my white dinner plates, washing them clean before the paint dries. We put bandages on vitamin bottles, counter tops, and, yes, even in books. The last time Jessie took a bath at our house, she used one of her rubber frogs as a squirt gun and, aiming at our dog, Pandy, soaked the floor.

Pandy and I didn't mind a bit.

I have a high tolerance for disorder, especially since I get the house back after Jessie leaves. This is a luxury reserved for grandmas.

It's hard to explain my behavior. I'm not trying to encourage Jessie to be "naughty," although I'm aware it sometimes looks that way to my daughter. It's just that I sometimes feel so in tune with Jessie's wishes and impulses, and so childlike myself, I can't think of a reason *not* to want what she wants as much as she does.

Take the matches, for instance.

Jessie had such a wonderful birthday that she invented a new name for cakes: "Happy-to-Yous." The words "hot," "candus," and "matchuz" immediately entered her vocabulary.

It was Jessie's idea that I light the book of matches she found on the kitchen counter. She wanted to look at the flame, to move as close to it as she dared. Looking earnestly into my eyes, she wagged her finger under my nose as she warned, "No touch ... hot!" before blowing each tiny fire into a spidery wisp of smoke.

I entered into her concentration. I saw her evaluate the danger. And I shared Jessie's total satisfaction when our book of matches—and our interest—burned themselves at the same time.

How can I explain it? It takes a bonfire to impress me, but, under Jessie's gaze, a tiny cardboard stick bursting into flame was magic. In her single-minded intensity, I came alive. If I'd been all prudence and no play, I'd have missed an unforgettable experience.

I support most of the guidelines Jessie's parents have set for her. She goes to bed on time, has a minimum of sweets at my house, and knows that, whenever she cries here or at home, someone will say, "Put it into words" before responding. I set limits so that Jessie knows "No!" wherever she is. It's just that I keep remembering what my supervisor taught me the year I was aquatic director at a summer camp:

Before you say "No," always think, "Can I possibly say 'Yes?'" We want these kids to have a wonderful time.

That's my philosophy of grandmothering in a nutshell.

As a mother, Laura fosters Jessie's self-control. A generation away, I encourage her spontaneity—but not unselfishly. In Jessie's company I'm blessed to discover within myself an inexhaustible source of laughter, my lost innocence, and a delight in—okay, I'll say it—mischief.

An irresistible sprite keeps showing up inside me, wanting to play. As a grandmother, I can't help looking mature, but I've discovered an unexpected benefit at this stage of my life.

I get a *second* childhood.

Reprinted from *Family Puzzles*, a book collection of *Boston Globe* columns by Linda Weltner (Innisfree Press, 1998). Used with her kind permission.

67

Making Jeffrey's Best Day

by Frank Cooper

When three of my grandchildren acquired a half-grown mongrel, I agreed to help them build a doghouse.

As we began the project, I knew that keeping them involved was going to be a challenge. Much of my energy was spent calling them back to the job and finding parts of the project that could be handled by small children. I held to my initial determination that building this doghouse was to be a group project.

Early in the project, I had promised the grandkids that we would roast wieners in the backyard as soon as we finished painting the canine residence. Selecting three of the largest house-painting brushes I could find, I supervised the painting of our homemade structure.

Kids and paint. How could I have forgotten the potential mayhem that such a combination can create?

After cleaning up the paint mess—kids, brushes, carport—I suggested that we could probably eat earlier if we just asked Gramma to heat the wieners in water on the gas range. A pang of guilt came over me as I realized I was trying to weasel out of an earlier promise.

As Jamie, Jeffrey, and Kimberley looked on, I built a first-class fire in our backyard pit, whittled some roasting sticks, and prepared for the outdoor cooking event.

When we finished eating, I leaned back on the cool grass and watched the last flickering remnants of our fire. Six-year-old Jeffrey was leaning back against my chest, and I began to think about what it meant to be a grampa.

The silence was broken when Jeffrey quietly reflected, "Know what, Grampa?" And, without ever breaking his gaze at the dying embers, he continued, "This is the best day of my whole life."

After a few moments of continued silence, he glanced up and said, "Are you crying, Grampa? You've got a tear on your cheek."

Clearing my throat, I explained that it must have been from the smoke.

Reprinted from *USA Today* with the kind permission of the author, Frank Cooper. Frank and his wife, Arnene, have 20 grandchildren and make their home in Everett, Washington.

68

Playing Catch with Grandpa

by Ira Blumenthal

I have five children. Starting with the eldest, they are 24, 21, 14, 11, and 5 years of age. Unfortunately, my father had a stroke when my oldest daughter was only a year old. Because the stroke left my father with a severe speech problem and paralysis on the right side of his body, none of my kids ever *really* got to know their grandfather as the vibrant, spirited, energetic man he was. He had a very difficult time talking to his kids and grandkids, and he had no use of his right arm. When he walked he would limp and drag his right leg.

Oh, the children loved him. They loved him because of his kind and gentle nature. But they never had the opportunity to have many significant conversations with him, and they never truly *played* with their grandpa.

While a young man (before his stroke), my father had enjoyed a sports career as a minor league professional baseball player, and he had also been a star football player. His sports accomplishments were legendary within the family. But his grandchildren had never even had a "catch" with their grandpa, at least not until the summer of 1998 when two determined grandkids, a 14- and an 11-year-old, decided it was time to play "catch" with Grandpa.

While on a summer vacation trip to visit Grandma and Grandpa, my sons Eric and Jeffrey planned to toss a baseball with their grandpa. They had brought their baseball gloves and a ball; they were prepared.

We picked Grandpa up at his house and told him we were going out for a surprise adventure. We drove to a vacant parking lot (Grandpa would have had difficulty moving on grass with his paralyzed leg). He was given a glove to wear on his good left hand; the rest of the story is grandparent baseball history.

One son stood next to Grandpa while the other positioned himself 10 to 15 yards away. The ball was thrown. Grandpa caught the ball and flipped it to the grandson standing next to him (sort of a "designated thrower," I suppose), who would then toss the ball back to his brother.

At first, Grandpa was a little shaky at catching the ball. However, after only a few minutes he began catching, catching, and catching—just like in the old days. Yes, he was catching just like the father I remembered when I was a kid. I had always wanted my children to experience this part of their grandfather in action.

"Grandpa, you're really good!" young Jeffrey exclaimed in a state of both amazement and excitement.

All of us, including Grandpa, caught, cried, caught, cried, and caught some more. Playing catch with their 81-year-old grandpa, my dad, will be a baseball memory that will have a place in our family's Hall of Fame forever.

Ira Blumenthal is an Atlanta-based consultant to world-class clients. He is the author of *Ready, Blame, Fire!* (Griffin Trade Paperbacks, 1998). He is the president of CO-OPPORTUNITIES, a university instructor and public speaker. www.IraSpeak.com

69

Raspberries

by Padi Selwyn

My grandma Viola loved raspberries more than any other food in the world. She lived with my grandfather in a tall, brick apartment building in Forest Hills, New York, and could only buy raspberries during a brief 2-week period each year. Raspberries were not grown anywhere nearby, but, in late spring her neighborhood market would stock them.

The market sold the berries in those tiny gray cardboard boxes. The boxes were so small they would fit in the palm of your hand; they held about 20 berries. But those few berries cost as much as a three-pound chicken—a lot of money in those days.

Having lived through The Great Depression didn't make it easy for my grandmother to pay such a dear price for those raspberries. But she did allow herself one little box each year, and she ate them *very* slowly. She ate them all herself; she wouldn't share even one precious raspberry with my grandfather, Papa Sam.

It was Grandma's annual indulgence.

Years later my family and I moved from New York state to northern California, where we built our home on a few acres of fertile land. We have many fruit trees and continue to grow a large vegetable garden every year. As you can guess, we planted raspberry bushes, and, every year, we harvest a big crop of the berries my grandmother loved so much.

As my grandparents grew older they began to spend more and more time on the West Coast. They visited our family and other family members who had also migrated to "God's Country." On one particular trip they happened to arrive at the very height of the raspberry season. I took my children out to the bushes on the day my grandparents were visiting, and we picked an enormous bowl full of juicy, ripe, crimson raspberries.

When Grandma Viola and Papa Sam arrived, they hugged and kissed us all. Grandma emptied her shopping bag of home-baked date-and-nut bread and all the other presents they had brought. Then we sat her down at the table and told her we had a surprise for her. We made her close her eyes as we placed a huge bowl of freshly picked and glistening berries in front of her.

In unison we all shouted, "Open your eyes!"

When Grandma opened her eyes she stared for a moment, then cried out, "Oh my God! I've never seen so many berries all at once."

We insisted that all the raspberries were hers, and handed her a spoon.

"I couldn't *possibly* eat so many," she protested.

For the next hour she sat at our kitchen table explaining that there were just too many berries to eat. "I'll get sick from eating them, " she warned. She promised, "I need to save some for later."

But, all the while, she *kept* eating the berries. Protesting, complaining, and making excuses for her raspberry appetite, Grandma ate until every berry was gone; nothing was left at the bottom of the bowl but a crimson stain. Her lips and teeth were red with a mile-wide berry juice smile.

Grandma Viola died a few years later. By then she and Papa Sam had moved to a retirement community nearby, so we were able to have her funeral at a cemetery close to home. She died at a time when our raspberry bushes were not bearing. But, on the morning of her funeral, I went out into the garden to pick fresh flowers for her grave. To my amazement, one bush was laden with raspberries! I quickly called my children to help me pick the last raspberries we would ever pick for Grandma Viola.

At the end of the funeral service we passed a large silver bowl of raspberries from hand to hand, mourner to mourner. In honor of my grandmother each of us ate a few berries; the rest were scattered on her marble gravestone.

I think she would have liked that.

Every year, when our raspberries ripen, I am again reminded of the sweetness of the love my grandmother and I shared.

Padi Selwyn, MA, is a professional speaker and author. She looks forward to being a grandparent someday.

70

Understanding
by Tony Schiller

This is a favorite story about my father and his grandson.

We were on a family outing at the lake home of my parents. My brother and I had been charged with hauling his speedboat up to the lake so that all the nieces and nephews (the grandkids) could get their fill of water-skiing.

All the kids loved to water-ski and were taking advantage of every opportunity to get a turn. Everyone, that is, except Cole. He was the only one of the kids to refuse; he was adamant. We tried to persuade him, to encourage him to at least give it a try.

"No," he said. "I don't want to try. Just leave me alone!"

We spent the day on the lake and all the kids (except Cole) had a marvelous time gaining in their proficiency and enjoying the moment. We finished for the day and docked the boat.

It was obvious that Cole was not a happy camper. When Grandma asked him if he had skied with the others, he responded, "No; I didn't want to."

My dad (granddad to Cole) observed Cole's attitude without saying anything to him in front of the others. Later that evening, I overhead Dad talking to Cole in private.

"I know just how you feel, Cole," he said. "I was the same way when I was your age. It wasn't that I was afraid to do stuff, I just didn't want to do it out there in front of everyone. I liked to learn things in private. That was my way, Cole."

The young man was listening intently.

After some additional conversation, I heard my dad offer Cole an alternative. "I'll tell you what, Cole," he offered, "later, if you want to, I'll take you out in the boat, just the two of us, and we'll go over to the other side of the lake and give this skiing thing a try." Dad started to leave. "Let me know if you want to give it a try. Okay?"

Later, the two of them, grandfather and grandson, slipped out of the house. They were gone until almost sundown. We heard the boat purring toward the shore. Everyone rushed out to observe the return of the missing pair. We saw Cole go skiing right past us. He looked great, and just as confident as the others.

Dad looped the boat back and brought it in. They walked up from the shore acting as if it were no big deal. I couldn't help thinking that my 75-year-old dad was a pretty cool dude. Smart, too.

I was proud of both of them.

Tony Schiller is a World Champion Triathlete and a speaker who draws powerful lessons from a lifetime in competition through his inspiring and humorous presentations on the Breakaway Mindset.

71

Surprise Package

by LIBBYLOVE Griffin

Grandma decided it was time to visit her daughter and granddaughter. They lived a nation apart; Grandma in North Carolina, daughter and granddaughter all the way across the country in California. She also decided on her mode of transportation: the Redeye Special, a long, weary, but less expensive trip. This meant that she would arrive during those wee (sometimes referred to as "ungodly") hours of the morning.

The airplane part of the journey was completed without incident and with only the usual inconveniences associated with any redeye flight. Just before dawn, the airport taxicab dropped off the worn and nearly exhausted grandma in front of her daughter's home. As she knew exactly where the front door key was hidden, both Grandma and her huge, overstuffed backpack made an uneventful and quiet entry.

Once inside, and not wanting to awaken anyone, Grandma, now totally wiped out, found an open spot on the floor for her and the backpack, eased herself down, and sprawled out into instant sleep.

Shortly thereafter, Grandma found herself being awakened by a gentle, but persistent, little finger that was repeatedly lifting her eyelid.

Grandma remained perfectly still, and did not move or raise her head from the arm she had used as a pillow. But she was quite aware that there were two little girls kneeling beside her; they were engaged in active conversation.

The first little girl, pointing to the heap on the floor, asked, "What is that? I've never seen anything like it before."

Grandma recognized her granddaughter's voice. The girl answered the question with obvious delight: "That's a grandmother!"

Later there were lots of hugs, kisses, and laughs.

LIBBYLOVE Griffin is the author of two books, a professional speaker, and the mother of nine. She is "Granny Biddy" to 25 grandchildren, and "Granny the Great" to 3 great-grandchildren.

72

Old-Fashioned Love

by Thelma Wells

My great-grandmother was a stickler for obedience. When she told me to do something—that's exactly what she meant for me to do. I vividly recall my 8th-grade prom. She told me to be home by 11:00 p.m. My grandfather, Daddy Lawrence, drove my date and me to the prom. My date's older brother was to bring us home.

When the prom was over, my date's brother remembered he had failed to turn out the lights at his place of employment when he closed for the night. He was terrified that his boss would find out. He decided that he had to make the 45-minute trip (each way) to turn out the lights.

We tried to telephone Granny from the YMCA to tell her we would be later getting home, but she was either on the telephone or a neighbor was using the line. (In those days we had a *party line*, a telephone line that was shared by two or more households. This was a pretty common arrangement in the 50s.)

It seemed as if we drove for days to reach the place where he worked. When we finally arrived, we went inside the building and tried our best to call Granny again. This time the phone rang but she did not answer. I was a nervous wreck. I was also scared to death and crying silently. I knew what awaited me when I got home; the thought had me petrified.

It seemed like forever, but we finally got home. Granny was standing on the curb in front of the drive that led up to the house. She was so angry she could barely speak. She gritted her teeth through a frown; there were tears in her eyes, and there was anger in her spirit.

In the strongest tone she could muster, Granny ordered, "Young man—you go home. Thelma; get in the house —NOW!"

It was all over. My short life had come to an end; Granny was going to kill me. I tried my best to explain what had happened, but nothing budged her. She wouldn't speak to me or even look at me. Granny just sat there in her tall, cane-backed rocking chair on our screened-in porch and refused to have anything to do with me.

I cried all night; I hated that she wouldn't speak to me. Never before had there been a situation where I was unable to talk to Granny. She had always listened before and allowed me to explain. Now she was shutting me out—not even looking my way. I couldn't stand it! What was I going to do? Perhaps wait it out? Waiting seemed to be the best plan.

The next day I told Granny what had happened, and asked her to please talk to my date's brother. I explained that we had tried to call her from the YMCA before we left, and also that we had tried to call again from his job site. Finally she agreed to speak with the brother. To this day, I don't know if she ever really forgave me for terrifying her so.

Now a mother and a grandmother myself, I think I realize how she felt. I was nearly 3 hours late coming home from a place only eight or nine blocks away, and I was with people my Granny had never met. She must have imagined everything that could have possibly happened to me. I'm sure she had visions of me getting beat up, in a wreck, in the hospital, maybe even doing something terribly wrong, or possibly dead. There were probably no limits to her thoughts of hurt, harm, or danger—a terrible experience for Granny.

Granny eventually came to realize that I did not disobey her deliberately. After several days, she began looking at me with tenderness in her eyes and touching me with loving arms. We were laughing and talking again. I was so pleased—and relieved.

I learned so many things from that experience, things I would never want to relearn. I learned how very deeply Granny had been hurt. I never wanted to do anything that would put her through that again; and I never did.

I learned that she was wise enough not to scold me or hit me while she was angry, a lesson that helped me in dealing with my own children. I learned that her love for me was so strong that she truly cared where I was, whom I was with, what I was doing, and how I was getting along. Granny's love was not superficial; it was the closest thing to God's love for his children that I could imagine.

I learned that my love and sensitivity for her grew as I watched her suffer over me, and I learned to keep her informed about where I was or where I was going to be. If I was going to be late, I knew to call (a practice I kept even after I was grown and married).

Thank you Granny for caring enough to take me into your home and heart when I was only 2 years old. Thank you for raising me to be an educated and productive person. Thank you for helping me to become a person who loves the Lord. I have tried my best to emulate your fine attributes in the living of my own life. You are the single most influential woman in my life.

Granny, you are the best. I love you.

Thelma Wells is the author of *God Will Make a Way* and *What's Going On, Lord?* (Thomas Nelson, 1998, 1999). She speaks to thousands at Women of Faith conferences throughout America.

73

Mamie and the Emerald Earrings

by Nan Andrews Amish

When I was a toddling 1-year-old, I was the instrument that renamed my grandmother. Somehow, with my limited language ability, I couldn't get the "grandmother" part quite right. It came out "Mamie" every time. The name stuck. All the younger relatives and most friends picked up on "Mamie"; it became her name, or nickname, if you will.

Mamie was filled with wonderful stories from her youth. One of our favorites was her story about some emerald earrings.

My grandfather (her husband) had given her a pair of emerald earrings as a present. He had received a big promotion from his company, and he wanted Mamie to share in his joy. The earrings were exquisite and very expensive (even for someone who had received a nice promotion). Mamie was touched by his gesture, and was excited to wear the earrings the very next day to a Christmas party.

The Christmas party was at the home of one of my grandfather's work associates. The home had a swimming pool, with Christmas decorations floating on top of the water. Very posh! Guests were served a special champagne-and-fruit punch. My grandfather duly warned Mamie not to drink too much punch; it was more potent than it tasted.

Well, Mamie didn't drink a lot of the punch, but she ate liberally of the fruit floating in it! Little did she realize that the fruit had soaked up the champagne. So, amply filled with her fruit supplement, she set out to admire the host's decorations. She leaned out over the pool to admire the floating decorations, and, as fate would have it, one of the emerald earrings fell into the pool. (She wasn't even aware that the earring had fallen until my grandfather brought it to her attention.)

What followed can best be described as lots of fuss and commotion. First, everyone joined in the search, gazing down into the pool, searching for the missing jewel. Someone finally saw something sparkling and everyone became excited. What to do now?

The butler came to the rescue, fully attired in his swimsuit to rescue the lost earring. My grandmother was mortified over the fuss she had caused, and my grandfather was equally displeased with the fuss, but also with my grandmother, who was obviously *drunk*. After all, he had hoped to make a good impression.

In order to prevent future losses, the earrings were sent to the jeweler the next day to be converted from "clip-on" to "pierced," and Mamie had her ears pierced to wear them (the earrings were also insured—just in case). She went to many other parties after that. She never lost another earring, and she *didn't* eat anymore fruit from the punch. After my grandfather passed away, Mamie only wore the emerald earrings on very special occasions.

No one in our family had pierced ears except Mamie. As she advanced in years, she would often hint that my mother and I needed to get our ears pierced so that, when she died, those emerald earrings would not end up in someone's swimming pool.

I really wanted my mother to have the emerald earrings, because Mamie had promised them to her. But as the favorite granddaughter, I was afraid the earrings might come to me directly if I pierced my ears first. My mother was not at all interested in having her ears pierced.

I decided to take matters into my own hands. I was tired of losing my own earrings. It was getting expensive to replace every other pair. So, for my mother's birthday, I bought her a pair of gold pierced earrings. When she opened them and realized what she had, she rolled her eyes with a gaze that said, "You know full well I don't have pierced ears." I did not need to respond. My mother knew I was trying to push her into piercing her ears, and she was having none of it. "If God had wanted us to have pierced ears we would have been born with extra holes in our heads," was one of her frequent comments on that subject.

My mother was annoyed that I had wasted good money on a pair of earrings she would never wear. She was so peeved that she told several of her colleagues at work that I was being a pain in the you-know-what. She told them that I knew full well she didn't have pierced ears, and that my attempt to influence her would not work.

Her colleagues were used to hearing good stories about me, and about how "smart" I was. Something was not adding up, so they asked my mother, "Why would she do *that*? She must have a reason; Nan is a smart girl."

My mother then related to them the story of Mamie and the emerald earrings. They all had a good laugh about "Boozy Grandma." But they decided I was on the right track, and, knowing my mother wouldn't make a fuss to them, they gave her several more pair of pierced earrings the next day.

She had her ears pierced the same week, much to Mamie's delight.

When Mamie passed away, my mother inherited the emerald earrings. She enjoys wearing them on those special occasions. When anyone comments on their beauty, she tells them the story about "Boozy Grandma" (a nickname my grandmother was never able to shake).

I had my ears pierced a year or so later so I wouldn't be losing my earrings—especially in swimming pools. I can now wear beautiful earrings without a thought of losing them. Each day, as I select a pair to wear and put them on, I think for a moment about my Mamie and her emerald earrings. I laugh a little at all of us.

Who would ever think that just having two holes in your head would continually stimulate such fond and loving memories?

Nan Andrews Amish, MBA, is a professional speaker, consultant, and coach. She specializes in leadership and organizational effectiveness. (800) 858-1750.

74

The Sign in the Store Window
by Etta Sutton Turner

It was Sunday, but it wasn't just *any* Sunday. It was my 80th birthday and my father had come to help celebrate. Papa and Marie, my stepmother, had driven 275 miles from Stockdale, Texas, to my home in Dallas just to be there for the occasion. Frankly, not many folks get to have their father show up for their 80th birthday. It was quite special for me.

As I entered the church sanctuary for the worship service that morning, Papa, Marie, and my husband were already seated. After I took my seat with my family, our minister of music came by to greet us.

Papa explained that he and Marie had come because it was my birthday. The minister of music asked which birthday I was celebrating. It never dawned on me that he might use my family and my birthday in an anecdote before the service began.

The members of the choir came in and took their places. A hush fell over the crowd as the 400+ folks in the congregation awaited the beginning of the service. But instead of leading the choir in the usual opening chorus, the minister of music stepped up to the microphone near the pulpit.

"Not long ago I was walking down the street when a sign in a store window caught my attention," he shared. "In large letters that sign read: 'Credit allowed to 80-year-olds only when accompanied by their father.'" The minister of music then went on to recognize my special birthday and my special birthday guest, noting that, indeed, I would be one of precious few who would ever qualify for credit in *that* store.

My father lived only 2 more years after that. Had he lived only 9 weeks longer, I would have been there to help him celebrate his 101st birthday.

Papa was dear to me. I feel truly blessed to be a member of his family, a family for which he had such an enduring love.

Etta Sutton Turner continues to live in Dallas, Texas, her home for many years. Her father must have passed on some pretty good genes, because Etta is now in her 90s and still going strong. She attributes the quality of her long life to faith, family and friends.

Credit allowed to
80-year-olds ONLY
when accompanied
by their father.

75

Grandma Does Not Have Enough to Do

by Joanne Wallace

When my granddaughter, Fallon, was 3-and-a-half years old she came to visit me for a couple of days. Because it is difficult for me to have all eight grandchildren visit at once, I usually try and take them one at a time. That way, I can spend a couple of days with each of them just doing things they will enjoy. I love this one-on-one time and try to make it extra special. We talk by the hour, play games, go shopping, and watch movies. But most of all—we laugh.

After two days of hilarious fun and laughing together, it was time for Fallon to go home. On the day I was to take her home, I kept telling her how wonderful she had been, and how much fun I had had with her. She seemed to drink in all the attention. Fallon listened closely when I said how much I would miss her and how I hoped she would come back to visit soon.

Although Fallon is not an overly talkative child, I could tell she was unusually quiet as we made the hour-and-a-half drive back to her house. Her furrowed brow and concentrated expression told me that something was troubling her; she was in deep thought about it. It was obvious she was working on a solution to a very knotty problem.

With her 3-year-old mind working overtime, Fallon suddenly pronounced her solution. With great compassion and sincerity she said, "I wish you had a kid like me!"

"What?" I thought. Where did she come up with that? Hoping to validate her feelings, I smiled and chuckled a bit as I said, "Well, I wish I had a kid like you too!"

My response did not satisfy her; it only seemed to provoke a *more* worried look. I gathered Fallon was trying to figure out how to give me a kid like her. But I wasn't sure just why.

"Why do you want Grandma to have a kid like you?" I asked her.

"Because then you would not cry all day and be lonely when I am not there!" she exclaimed with true concern.

Aha! *Now* I understood. She had translated my missing her into a paralyzing grief that made it difficult for me to function. What a burden for her!

"So do you think Grandma cries all day when you are not around?"

"Yes."

Still chuckling to myself, I gently let her know that, as much as I missed her, I did do a few other things during the day! She seemed relieved by this, and was happy to know that I could plan and do many things between the times I spent with her.

As I reflect on this incident, I am reminded of how we sometimes view God as a genie in a lamp, inactive until we rub the lamp and ask for our wishes to be granted. What a poor life God would have if He were just sitting around waiting for us to have time to spend with Him.

But that is not the reality at all. Yes, He misses us when we are away from Him, but He is not incapacitated or "on-hold" during our time away. *We* are the ones who miss out when we do not spend time with Him.

God has planned many activities for us and wants to shower us with His blessings. As for me, I don't want to miss *any* of those blessings. Like Fallon, I want God to "have a kid like me" around at *all* times. I know God can function without me, but I do not function well without Him!

And if you hardhearted, sinful men know how to give good gifts to your children, won't your Father in heaven even more certainly give good gifts to those who ask him for them?"
—Matthew 7:11

Joanne Wallace is an author of nine books and a speaker for Christian conferences. This story is reprinted (with permission) from her book *As Refreshing as Snow in the Hot Summertime: Stories to Energize Your Faith, Lighten Your Spirit, and Deepen Your Hope* (Wallace, 1998). Contact: 1825 Coast Avenue, Lincoln City, OR 97367. (541) 994-3550.

76

Real Longevity

by Troy Crabtree

Matthew, my 3-and-a-half-year-old grandson, was seated with me in one of those old-fashioned backyard swings. We were gently moving back and forth in silent, rhythmic unison. Both of us were deep in our thoughts, and were fully enjoying the "just being together" part of a very wonderful and special relationship.

It was Matthew who finally broke the silence. He lifted his young, sparkling eyes to meet my older "been-around-a-long-time" eyes.

"Popie, I know you're getting older and one day you're gonna die." Then he put his little hand over his heart and continued. "But you'll never really die, Popie, because you'll always live right here in my heart."

Suddenly my eyes were not as clear (and certainly not as dry) as they had been just moments before. I felt my heart nearly bursting with love for my grandson.

Matthew had just guaranteed my immortality.

Troy Crabtree, a Durham, North Carolina native, is a retired industrialist who now has ample time to spend being a loving grandfather, father and husband.

77

A Day with Grandpa
by Jim Moore

I pulled the hood of the Mackinaw over my head to protect myself from the chill. Feeling that autumn cold penetrate my bones was just part of being in Pennsylvania at this particular time of year. The Penn State homecoming parade was about to start. As always, I looked forward to the floats and the marching bands. But the highlight for me was the exciting appearance of the Nittany Lion (Penn State's mascot).

I remembered that it had been a truly wonderful day. It began with a neat trip over to State College, through the farmlands and forests of Pennsylvania, in Grandpa's new Chevrolet. It was our custom to visit the trout farms near Bellefonte on the way. Then we would drive right past the Rockview State Penitentiary (which had always intrigued me). At trip's end, we would drive into town and find a parking place in the crowded downtown area.

Once parked, we would start shopping around in the variety of stores and shops across from the campus. We were searching for a new toy for me to take home.

Of course, no visit to the Penn State campus was complete without a trip to the Creamery for an ice cream cone. In my memory, I can still taste the wonderful flavors; picking just one was always so difficult.

The day after the parade we would take in the homecoming football game. Going to any football game with Grandpa was always exciting. I recall the feeling of spending time with someone who really loved me—who enjoyed just being with me. That feeling always made those annual trips so special. As I clutched my Grandpa's hand, I felt the cold being replaced by a warming glow of just being with someone very special.

I looked up at my Grandpa, expecting to see his familiar face. Then I realized I wasn't looking up at all; I was looking *down*. Yes, down; I was looking into the radiant eyes of my own grandson, Hayden. I had been reliving those wonderful "Grandpa times" of years past. I had drifted back to when I was a boy.

Grandpa had shared so much love with me that I have found it easy to pass the tradition down to my own grandchildren. I am hoping that one day Hayden will be standing right here, waiting for the parade to begin, while holding yet another very special hand. They'll be busy creating more loving memories, keeping the tradition of love that binds grandparent and grandchild.

Jim Moore is founder and president of Moore Ideas, Inc. He specializes in performance and profit enhancement in retail operations. He is a professional speaker, author and consultant.

78

"Open the Door"

by Wayne E. Baughman

My mother was away for the day. My grandfather was in charge of the kids at our home. It was Grandpa, my younger brother Dick, and me.

Dick was outside riding his tricycle on the sidewalk. He was several houses down from our house when he had an accident that caused him to sail over the top of the handlebars. He came down on the sidewalk chin first; a bad fall. As he got up, Dick noticed that his chin was bleeding profusely. He ran for home.

Grandpa was there for just such a purpose, to offer help and consolation. But, for no reason he could ever explain, Dick ran into the house, to the bathroom, and shut and locked the door.

Grandpa pleaded with him to open the door. He even threatened Dick if he didn't open the door. It was the only time I can remember my grandfather being really angry. He was also frustrated; he wanted to help Dick, but my brother would not open the door. I suppose he was afraid.

All afternoon, Grandpa pleaded with Dick to open the door, but it stayed shut and locked. It was not until my mother got home that Dick finally opened the door. The cut on Dick's chin was long and deep; it could have used some stitches. But by then the bleeding had stopped, so they just left it alone.

My brother carries that scar on his chin to this day. Grandpa carried it for a long time as well, always encouraging us to trust him in time of need.

I always did.

Wayne E. Baughman's business, Creative Presentations, assists people in controlling the fear of speaking, helps them to make better business presentations, and to be more creative.

79

The Sweetest Sound

by Jerry Coffee

When my granddaughter, Amy, was about 7, I took her with me and Susan to a meeting on Maui where I was speaking. Her main interest was the big water slide at the pool, but she did come to hear me speak. It was a very family-oriented meeting, and Susan and Amy were sitting in the front row.

In the context of my opening remark I introduced them, and mentioned how special this was for me in that it was Amy's first opportunity to hear her "Bapa" speak.

The program went well, the rest of the day was fun-filled, and we returned to Oahu that evening. En route, I asked Amy if she'd had a good time. She said emphatically that she had. I asked further, "Did you enjoy my speech?"

Amy nodded her approval. "What part do you remember the most?" I asked.

"The part where you said *my* name!"

Just another reminder of that old rule of conversational connection; the most pleasant sound is that of our own name!

Retired Navy Captain Gerald L. Coffee was, for over 7 years, a Prisoner-of-War in North Vietnam. His story and his book, *Beyond Survival* (Putnam, 1990), have been inspiring audiences of thousands for over 25 years. 800-840-1776.

80

The Upside-Down Bath

by Al Walker

I was very close to my maternal grandparents—Mommee and Pop. This is a story my grandmother loved to tell on me.

I was about 5; Mommee was bathing me in an old #10 steel washtub. She'd placed the tub in the middle of the bedroom floor, and put enough water in it to lather me and rinse me off.

During the bath, I would put my hands on the sides of the washtub and sort of rock it back and forth. Mommee would tell me to quit, and I would ... for a few seconds. Soon, I was right back to rocking the tub.

When she had finished bathing me, she realized she had not brought a towel; she stood to go get one.

"Now don't you go to rocking that tub while I'm gone," she warned. "You'll turn it over and spill that water all over my floor."

"Hmmm ... these can actually be turned over?" I remember thinking as she left the room. And I proceeded to do just that. All the water, plus a very naked 5-year-old, went everywhere!

Mommee heard the commotion and rushed back into the bedroom just in time to see the last drops of soapy water drip onto her beautiful, hand-woven carpet, then onto the hardwood floors underneath.

She was upset! Mommee jerked me up and took me out to the front porch. She took a long, slender limb from a nearby shrub and started whacking away on my bare bottom and the back of my legs, all the while admonishing me for disobeying her.

Then she realized that she was whipping up on her oldest and most favorite grandchild. She felt terrible about it (according to the way she related the story later on). For the rest of her days, Mommee would tell that story to anyone who'd listen, and always ended it by saying that I was the *only* grandchild she's ever punished. And I remember always thinking, "Well, lucky ol' me!"

But it turned out I *was* the lucky one. Mommee spent the rest of her life encouraging me and doing all she could for me. I guess it was her way of making up for the spanking she'd given me.

Truth is, *I* was the big winner on that deal.

Al Walker, CSP, CPAE and Cavett Award recipient is a professional speaker whose humor and powerful message has kept audiences laughing for over 20 years. He's known as "a big man with a big message." Anyone who has ever seen and heard him agrees.

81

If You Don't Plan, You Won't Go

by Fire "Captain Bob" Smith

If you don't plan, you won't go. I have concluded that folks need to get away on a regular basis. It is not optional; it's mandatory. We need to do it while we are alive and able. It happens all too fast. One day we are living; the next day we aren't, and our friends go over to someone's house and eat potato salad. Only, we won't be there.

I can hear it now: "One of these days ... some day ... when the time is *right*." But sometimes "some day" never happens. Plan a trip now; put it on your calendar. You will enjoy the anticipation of going, and you'll have lasting memories.

My wife, Harriet, and I were planning a trip to Hawaii. Six weeks before we were scheduled to leave, we went to visit my wife's boss. Steve was a patient at Stanford University Hospital. He was only 48 and at the very top of his game—a wealthy tycoon in commercial real estate. He had a liver tumor and was fighting for his life.

During that visit, Steve gave us a message: "Don't wait! You never know what's going to happen." I took it to heart.

The next day I arranged flights to Hawaii for our two sons and their families. I didn't tell Harriet; it would be a surprise. She would have a full week to relax before the boys and their families joined us, and she wouldn't have to worry about all the details.

Three days before we were to spring a big Mother's Day surprise on her, Harriet and I were walking on the beautiful beach at the north end of Kauai. The surprise almost happened then and there. Walking just 50 feet in front of us was our son Rob, daughter-in-law Nancy, and our 3- and 5-year-old grandsons, Christian and Trevor.

"There goes the surprise," I thought. But she *never* saw them! I whisked her up to the edge of the beach. While she relaxed, I watched our grandsons snorkel.

She never knew.

On Mother's Day, Harriet and I were enjoying our drinks while gazing at the sunset over Bali Hai. Suddenly Harriet said, "Look, Bob, those two little guys over there look just like Christian and Trevor." (Good reason, too; their grandmother had purchased the outfits they were wearing).

The boys came over with flower leis for their Gramma and Grandpa. "Let the games begin!" I said. The time we all spent together over the next week was a time of real magic.

One day Harriet said, "Today is Girls' Day Out." It turned out pretty special for the boys too, especially Grandpa. It was a time for me to go to the beach with my two sons and my two grandsons.

It just doesn't get any better than that.

After hearing that message from Steve, Harriet and I are sharing even more with the kids. We are now big into making memories. Nothing else is as important. We're doing the things that really count—while we can do them.

But if you don't plan, you won't go.

Fire "Captain Bob" Smith is a recognized expert and speaker on stress, communications and relationship skills. He is the author of *Fire Up Your Communication Skills* (Code 3 Publications, 1997) www.eatstress.com

82

The Boy in My Life

by Linda Weltner

My granddaughter was making regular appearances in this column by the time she was 2 years old. In contrast, I've barely breathed a word about my 2-year-old grandson, Danny. I see him all the time. I love him to pieces, but, as the mother of two girls, I wasn't adequately prepared to have a boy in my life.

At least, not *this* boy.

I can confess now that, at first, I thought Danny might be autistic. I kept silent, but here was this baby, home from the hospital a whole week, and he wasn't making eye contact. I remember the instant connection Jessie and I had made from birth, but Danny stared into space or looked away when I placed myself in his line of sight. I quietly called a pediatrician and received his reassurance that this was normal behavior.

Danny *did* eventually look at me, but not with the same fervor with which he eyed trucks and trains. When Jessie and I played together, she focused on our interaction. Danny, on the other hand, was totally engrossed in his tasks. Playing in a sandbox, he'd be so focused on sifting and shoveling that I often felt tempted to pick up a book. To Danny, the interpersonal seemed incidental.

I always told Jessie stories while we drove in the car, and she always paid rapt attention. With Danny, as I paused for effect after the wolf said, "I'll huff, and I'll puff ... ," he'd shout excitedly, "Truck!" Soon, all our interactions on the road went something like this:

Danny: "Truck."

Nana: "Oooh, a big truck."

Danny: "Big truck."

This was his idea of a truly fascinating conversation.

I could understand why Danny liked tunnels, and pushing his cars in and out, in and out, of tunnels. I accept that anatomy is destiny, but what is there about large-wheeled vehicles that hooks boys? From my point of view, what is even vaguely interesting about them?

On our morning together each week, I'd take Danny to watch some nearby construction because I knew he loved it. I'd feel his body come alive with a mixture of fear and delight as he watched backhoes and bulldozers at work.

"What about this thrills him so?" I would ask myself. "Will I *ever* be able to empathize?"

That winter, however, something changed. Perhaps it was a natural progression, an inevitable result of his growing older. Perhaps attentive parents and a large and loving extended family socialized it into him. In any case, one day I was pushing a small metal jet onto the runway of his airport. The next moment, Danny was driving a busload of imaginary people out to meet my plane.

Bingo! I got so excited that we were playing together that I scooped him up and danced him all around the house.

Two days later, he met me at the door screaming. "Nana! Nana!"

I can't say whether nature or nurture has made Danny who he is, or whether his task orientation is a facet of his personality or his gender, but learning to share my grandson's interests has been a big stretch for me. I've had to overcome my initial reluctance, then go through the motions of sharing Danny's enthusiasm until I could muster some of my own.

My brother lent us his son's Brio train collection, and I was actually quite proud of the elaborate train layouts I built with Danny each week. And I created awesome obstacle courses for the Matchbox cars that manage to survive their trips around a loop of plastic raceway.

These days, Danny and I drive to the train station and tremble when the train roars in. We make roads for trucks in the sandbox and enjoy the sound of Sergeant Murphy's motorcycle on

Danny's *Touch 'n' Listen* storybook. I've interested him in digging up worms from my yard and feeding them to my friend Gail's chickens. He lies across a swing, and I twist him around and around until he twirls through the air like a Frisbee.

I get a definite kick out of being with Danny. Grandchildren, they say, keep you young.

This one's introducing me to my inner boy.

Reprinted from *Family Puzzles*, a book collection of *Boston Globe* columns by Linda Weltner (Innisfree Press, 1998). Used with her kind permission.

<u>83</u>

Near Perfection

by Muriel Yilmaz

I looked down at his small face. I observed his mouth with those delicate but finely detailed lips. I smelled his sweet breath. I was astonished at how much love I felt for this tiny boy—my first grandchild. The first son of my second son.

This little fellow had taken us by surprise. His very conception was a surprise, as was the timing of his birth. He was born 3 weeks premature, weighing in at 4 pounds and 14 ounces. Even now, at 3 weeks, he is just a little over 5 pounds.

As an expectant grandmother, I had flown from my home in Washington, DC, to Arkansas to attend the baby shower for my daughter-in-law. After my arrival, however, she was placed on bedrest due to some potentially very serious complications for her and the baby.

During my stay, I went with her to the hospital for her frequent check-ups. I helped check her blood pressure, and I was able to listen to the baby's heartbeat. I watched the monitor with awe and fascination. After a short visit, I decided to return home and await further developments. I arrived home only to find that she was on the way back to the hospital to have the baby.

He was born the following day.

Obviously my timing wasn't the greatest; I missed the delivery. But as I looked down at this little miracle, I was consumed with love. I felt so much love it was like he was my own child.

I especially loved those quiet, intimate moments when we were alone —the times when I had convinced his mom and dad to go out and spend some time together. I would be all alone with *my* baby, and I would find myself saying "Mommy" to him instead of "Grandma." I would lie him down on my chest and let him sleep for hours. I never realized I could sit still for such a long time.

I had never found that kind of time when my children were small; there was always too much to do. I had dinner to prepare, clothes to wash, a house (and me) to straighten up—all before my husband got home.

With this little boy, I was finding a relationship that was near perfection. As a grandma, I could enjoy him totally. I also knew that, when his parents returned, I could hand him over to them, satisfied he would get the best of care. I could offer my "two cents" worth of advice and still leave trusting that all would go well, even if I wasn't there. I could rest easy and sleep through the night, knowing my grandson would be properly fed and cared for. Oh, the benefits of grandmother-hood.

I am fortunate and thankful that I have a wonderful relationship with my daughter-in-law and her parents (who only live an hour or so away, and can visit the baby almost any time). They allow me to monopolize "my baby" when I'm there. The ability to love him unconditionally makes for a blessed and relaxed trip.

Although I'm a "long-distance" grandma, I see my new grandson every day in my mind's eye. Many nights I fall asleep seeing his face. (Since I'm now alone, his vision brings me great joy and comfort.) I have thoughts of nuzzling his neck and kissing his head as if he were there on my chest, between my breasts. I've decided nothing can compare to the "packaged sweetness" of this first grandbaby. Nothing.

It's going to happen again—soon. My second grandchild is due in October; I am eager for the arrival. My oldest son and his wife live less than an hour from me, but her parents live in Finland. They will need me. I am blessed with another great relationship; they look for my presence and my support.

My youngest son is studying to be a pediatrician. He's not married yet, but he has a great love for children. I know that he and his wife-to-be will have lots of kids for me to love also.

That's who I am.

Muriel Yilmaz is a success-centered motivational speaker, trainer and career coach. Dubbed "The Queen of Success" by WWRC Radio, her focus is on the spiritual side of our lives.

84

I'm Going to be a Nana
by Kathy Zullo

After I received the news from Allison that I was going to be a nana, my reaction of, "Wow, this is great!" turned into, "Oh, my God. Now what do I do? What kind of grandmother do I want to be? Can I, should I, be like my Grandma Lang?"

My grandmother was wonderful. She was a large woman who lived on a farm and could do just about everything. She patiently taught me how to cook, knit, quilt, sew, and garden.

After Allison's call I wondered, "Am I going to have to do all those things for *my* grandchildren?" I don't even like baking cookies. Sewing? Knitting? It's cheaper to *buy* the clothes. And I never was much good at those things anyway.

But then I realized a grandmother's love and attraction to her grandchildren is as natural and deep as the love she felt toward her own babies. Some ways of showing that love will always remain the same. But as times change, so do grandparenting styles.

So I don't bake cookies. I love to travel. What fun it will be to take the grandchildren to the Keys, Manhattan, and Disney World. We'll introduce them to our interests, like archaeology, photography, and canoeing. We'll outfit them with backpacks and hike along the Appalachian Trail, climb rocks on the Blue Ridge Mountains, and raft down the Nantahala.

But maybe I'll make cookies after all. For some reason, cookies and grandmothers *still* seem to go together.

Reprinted from the book, *The Nanas and the Papas (A Boomer's Guide to Grandparenting)* by Kathryn and Allan Zullo. Used with the permission of The Wordseller, Inc. and Andrews McMeel Publishing (1998).

85

A Grandmother's Dream

by Aleta Pippin

Farleigh, my granddaughter, was born on August 7, 1997. I feel a special connection with her, having dreamed of her birth the very night she came into this world.

My daughter Melissa woke me at 2:30 a.m. I answered the phone with these words: "So you're ready. I just dreamed that Farleigh was born. I heard her crying." A little later a beautiful baby girl was born, the journey complete.

The following story came to me after witnessing the miracle of birth—Farleigh's birth. This could have been her story:

I feel pressure against me! What is this? What's happening to my little world? Wasn't it bad enough that my world has dramatically shrunk over the last several months? Now it's uncomfortable, too.

When I was really small, I had plenty of room to move about. I was free to move like a scuba diver with life support. Rather than an out-of-body experience, I was having an inner-body experience—floating about with all that I needed to survive attached to my belly.

I loved that feeling of floating; there was no restriction. I could go around and around, and even spend days standing on my head—if I wanted to. Then I began to notice my world slowly shrinking; no more free and easy floating anymore. I wanted more space.

Humph ... ah ... that feels better. Kicking, I can make a little more room.

What are those things resting on me? I can feel them stroking my world. It feels like loving energy. Could it be God? What's that sound? I hear a constant and rhythmic "da-dum-da-dum-da-dum." Is that the sound of God? I hadn't noticed it before.

There's another sound—a soft sound that seems to be directed at me. It must be a voice sound, but I can't make out the words. I can hear a deeper voice too, and larger, stronger hands caressing my world.

God must have many faces.

What's that? Yikes; I'm being squeezed. My world has really gotten smaller these last few weeks. I've been standing on my head. One day I was floating around, but now I've ended upside-down with my head in this hole. My head—it's caught!

Ouch; there it goes again! Is this an earthquake. Now my whole world is moving. No place to hide; I can't get away!

I hear God's voice again. It sounds muffled—like some sort of grunting.

Ouch! Ouch! Ouch! My world is collapsing as I'm being pushed deeper into the hole. My head is really stuck now! Fingers—I keep feeling fingers around the crown of my head. They're pulling on me. No! Let me go! You're really messing up my world.

Hey, maybe I'm dying. I'm in a tunnel, just like everyone talks about—a long, dark tunnel.

Humph! My head's free now. Light! I must be in heaven.

My whole body's free now; God's holding me in his hands. But wait. He's sticking something into my nostrils and mouth. Air suddenly fills my lungs. What a feeling, air rushing in and out—a new sensation, a new rhythm.

Other hands are now holding me. Does God have a helper? These hands are rough; they're rubbing me all over with a piece of cloth. This isn't heaven; I remember now. I was in heaven and the woman named Melissa called to me. She wooed me and told me how wonderful it would be to live with her.

Wait; I'm being moved again. Yes, I can tell; I'm in the woman's arms. That touch is so familiar. It's just like God's touch when I was floating about in my previous world. And I feel the other, stronger, touch as well.

Home, at last.

Aleta Pippin is an author from La Jolla, California. She is the founder of "Inner Sources for Change," and is committed to assisting others to achieve more meaning in their lives.

86

Harvest Time in the Garden of Life

by Lillias Kidd

Jim and Jon Tiller, two of our grandsons, were born respectively in Virginia and North Carolina. You could say, however, that they both grew up in Durham, North Carolina, a pretty good place to grow up. The Tillers often came to visit, and something memorable almost always happened.

During one such visit, while the adults stood chatting outside, Jim spied a bushel of large tomatoes that had just been picked by his grandfather. "Ball!" he whispered (he was just beginning to talk), as he selected a tomato and threw it down the hill. Several more tomatoes rolled down the hill before I intervened to rescue the rest of the bushel.

Another episode involved Jon and his grandfather in the garden. Jon looked perplexed as his grandpa hoed the potatoes to the surface. "Pa-paw," he questioned, "what are your potatoes doing under all that dirt?"

Grandfather did his best to explain, but explanations are difficult when a youngster has seen potatoes come only out of a bag. Jon always had plenty of these kinds of questions; and Grandpa tried his best to answer them.

Sometimes Grandpa Kidd would take the boys (and maybe even an uncle or two) fishing at one of the country lakes about 30 miles from our place. They always had a great time. Jim and Jon often recall the time when one of their great-uncles fell into the water while trying to save the fish the boys had caught. Their stringer of fish was floating away from the boat, and, one way or another, he was going to retrieve it. What a splash!

My relationship with my grandsons has been equally close, though a bit different. It usually involves special things to eat (a unique role generally reserved for grandmothers). I especially liked to make homemade grape jelly from the grapes that the boys saw growing on our place. Many times, they even picked the grapes themselves (it's interesting how jelly made from those grapes always tasted better). They loved it. "When Grandma Kidd's jelly is not on the table, it's like eating at someone else's house," Jim would say. When Jon was just beginning to talk, he would toddle down the grocery aisle with his mom and check out the grape jelly on the shelves. "Grandma Kidd not make it," he would say.

Although Jim and Jon have always lived a good distance away, our fondness and affection for each other has remained strong. These "boys" are now in their mid-20s, and, because illness keeps us from visiting them, they call, visit, and send cards and even gifts. They return to us, in kind, what we shared with them.

Isn't that what love is really all about?

Lillias Kidd is a retired first grade teacher who taught in the mountains of Virginia. Five times a grandmother, Lillias and her husband, Ralph, have been married for 56 years.

<u>**87**</u>

The Wondrous Gift of "Begin Again"

by Linda Weltner

I'm stretched across my daughter's bed, feeding my grandchild. Jessie contentedly sucks away at the bottle I'm holding for her. At 4 months, she doesn't know much about the world, but her eyes, wide and unblinking, are locked on mine. When Jessie sleeps, I see her dad in the shape of her face and the color of her skin. But when she opens her eyes and stares into mine, I feel as if I am looking past the blue-gray irises and large dark pupils all the way into what Emerson called the Oversoul—"That within which every man's particular being is contained and made one with all others."

It isn't recognition I see there; Jessie hasn't placed me on her map yet, but there's contact and a merging of consciousness. I feel as if I could hang laundry on the beam of light that links the two of us. From these depths, Jessie radiates curiosity.

And I gaze back, empty of everything but the sight and delight of her.

With Jessie, I'm in the present, my mind uncluttered by thoughts of the past or future. A voice within whispers, "Now," riveting my attention to this child, this interaction, this magical moment, as if the concept of time had never been discovered. For these few hours, I have no chores, no errands, and no calls to return.

I am "babysitting," a word that gives no clue to its magic.

It is the wondrous gift of "begin again."

Much like an undeserved blessing, here comes another chance. Gone are the ingredients that made mothering so difficult: the long hours, the isolation, the fear of not doing the right thing. Gone is the exhaustion, the discipline, the panic of enforced confinement. Jessie's mom and dad can worry about how she turns out. As a grandmother, I can put my trust in what Emerson would call Jessie's "wise silence." There is nothing I *have* to teach her. I can measure her by what Emerson called "the soul's scale," ignoring the judgment of ordinary folks who cannot see her for the miracle she already is.

My job is simple: to enjoy the pressure of Jessie's grip as she wraps her fingers around mine, to inhale the sweet smell of her, to share her perfect happiness when she has drunk her fill of milk and Grandma's face. As her eyelids flutter down, I settle into a peaceful place I could never find on my own.

This bond that binds the generations is a sacred one. What I loved in my daughters, I love again in this small, trusting soul. The love that my husband and I gave to our daughters has gathered strength, traveling through them like a stream whose source and ultimate destination are forever hidden. In this moment, love because a tangible force as wide as an ocean, as varied as each of us is from one another.

"Jessie," I whisper to her, "welcome to my life. There is no greater pleasure I will ever know than to love you without expectation, without condition, and without restraint."

Reprinted from *Family Puzzles*, a book collection of *Boston Globe* columns, by Linda Weltner (Innisfree Press, 1998). Used with her kind permission.

88

"Stop and Fix It"

by Nan Leaptrott

My 3-year-old granddaughter was in the back seat; I was driving. We were on our way home and everything was relatively peaceful in the car. It was early evening; dusk had descended and night was coming. I was deep in thought, and Anna was busy looking out of the window as the world passed by.

Suddenly the silence was shattered! In a voice filled with both excitement and despair, Anna called out to me: "Stop and fix it. Oh, Grandnannie, stop and fix it!"

Fix? Fix what? I looked at Anna, searching for something wrong or out of place. She was safely strapped in her car seat alright, and I could see nothing wrong—nothing loose or broken. But she was obviously upset.

"What, Anna?" I inquired. "What would you like for me to fix?"

"The moon!" she quickly responded, gesturing into the sky. "The moon, Grandnannie; it's broken. Can't you see?"

In her world of brightly colored picture books and children's television shows, the moon is supposed to be big and round and golden where little children live. The moon she saw looking in at her through the car window was a pale half-moon that was hanging low in the evening sky. It didn't look anything like *her* moon. It was broken, and it was Grandnannie's job to fix it.

After all, grandmothers can fix anything.

Indeed, there are those days when my life is paled and half-filled with disappointment, unresolved problems, or just plain fatigue. I wish I could cry out to someone, "Fix my life!" Then I reflect for a moment, and realize there *is* someone. My heavenly Father is always there to help me if I just remember to ask. And, when something can't be fixed on the spot, He will give me the grace to bear it—until it can be fixed.

Nan Leaptrott, an internationally acclaimed authority on global business, is the author of *Rules of the Game! Global Business Protocol* (Thompson Executive Press, 1996). She can be reached at P.O. Box 776, Pinehurst, NC 28374.

89

Grandparent Comments by Grandkids

by Students of Cresset Christian Academy

The following children attend school at Cresset Christian Academy in Durham, North Carolina. They were asked to explain why they love their grandparents.

I love my grandma because she gets me toys and she gives me money for the carousel. I love my grandpa because he plays basketball with me. He also takes me to the movies, and we share popcorn. I love my grandma and grandpa because they love me."

—Amanda, second grade

I love my grandpa and my Mema because my grandpa takes me on tractor rides! I love my grandma because we do everything together!"

—Kristi, second grade

I love my Granny because she bakes chocolate pies with whipped cream and seven cherries on them."

—Anna, second grade

I love my grandma and my grandpa because they have a very big farm. I especially like my grandpa because he takes me to the train museum. I especially like my grandma because she takes me to the Museum of Art.

—Stuart, second grade

I love my Nana because she works at a nail salon. She gives me almost every color of nail polish. She also makes good cakes. She has three cats.

—Lydia, second grade

I love my Gran because she laughs with me all the time. She takes me shopping a lot. She'll buy me a Beanie Baby sometimes.

—J.B., second grade

I like my Nana because whenever I go to her house she gives me seashells, fixes me strawberries with whipped cream on top and always tells my brother to get off the TV when I wake up. But most of all I love her because she loves me and we can trust each other.

—Sarah, third grade

I love my Grandma because she buys me gifts every year.

—Matthew, third grade

I love my Grands because they are the best grandparents you could have, and they are always there.

—Alex, third grade

I love my Nannie because she is nice. She replaces my toys. Like one time I lost my Bun-Bun (bunny rabbit) and she replaced it. I love my Papa because every time he goes fishing he takes me with him. And, I just love them both.

—Abby, third grade

I love my Grammie and Grandpa because they love me. I know they love me because they care about me—they never forget me. They also write me once a week. When I was little my Grammie would play my favorite game, "Hide the Shells." She also would play "Ants" with me—I like that a lot, too. Grandpa builds dollhouses. He makes them for me and my cousins. He collects lots of things. I love it when I go to their house because they have a pool and cook great food!"

—Megan, fourth grade

I like my grandpa because he is full of energy. He will let me scare him when I shoot him with Nerf balls when he comes out of the room. I like my grandpa because I can talk him into anything and talk him out of anything.

—Saige, fourth grade

I love my grandparents because they are good Christians. They love God with all their hearts. My grandma plays the piano and my grandpa sings in the choir. They watch me when my parents are at work. My grandma lets me do anything and eat anything. They love me and take me to church. They are nice and worry when I worry, and are sad when I am sad. That's why I love my grandparents.

—Cassie, fifth grade

I love my grandparents 'cause they love me. I love my grandma 'cause she does a lot of things for me. I also love her 'cause she is very nice. I also love her 'cause she comforts me. I love my grandpa 'cause he likes to watch TV with me. I also love him 'cause he makes good company. I also love him 'cause he can make me feel happy. I love my Grandmomma 'cause she teaches me to do the right thing. I also love her 'cause she's always happy to hear from me. I also love her 'cause she takes care of me when I'm sick. I love my Granddaddy 'cause he's fun to be around. I also love him 'cause he teaches me to obey. I also love him 'cause he wants me to be safe.

—David, fifth grade

I love my grandma because ... she takes me places I like to go. And she gives me nice presents. Sometimes I spend the night at her house and in the morning we go to Bojangles. My grandma is really nice. I am thankful to have a nice grandma.

—Jordan, fifth grade

I love my grandparents because they are kind and loving. When I go to their house Grandma bakes pies and makes apple cider. My grandma is a very good cook and can sew very well. I love them very much.

—Barrett, fifth grade

I love my Granny because she always had time for me as I was growing up. She would bake biscuits and make delicious dumplings. She has gone to be with the Lord and I miss her dearly. She had 25 grandchildren and she always knew how to make each one of us feel so warm and loved. I will see her again and, who knows, we might have her dumplings on a cloud!

—Debra Melvin, elementary principal

Part Four

Portraits

T hese stories paint with words, resulting in a loved one's indelible image.

90

Nanny and the Story-Brusher

by Bobbie Richardson Sutton

Among my favorite childhood memories is one of "The Farm," a place where my mother's parents lived. Going to the farm was always filled with adventure. Nanny would pack a lunch for me, I would borrow a horse from the neighbor, and I would ride around the farm on great adventures.

One of my favorite stops on this horseback journey was the stock tank near the house (in Texas these tanks were dug to capture and hold water for the livestock, but they also did marvelous double-duty as a fishin' hole and swimming pool). I'd sit on the fishing dock and eat my lunch (always sharing a little of it with the perch). Then I'd climb back on the horse and continue the adventure.

But my most favorite times were when I stayed the night at the farm. In the evenings near bedtime, I would brush Nanny's long hair while she told me wonderful stories. As long as I brushed, the stories would come.

Two stories stand out to this day. One explained how she met Papa, my grandfather. It was at a church bazaar. The single young ladies all made picnic lunches, and the young men bid on them (which meant that the highest bidder got not only the lunch, but the lunchtime company of the young lady who made it). Well, Nanny knew whom she wanted to share her lunch with—and it *wasn't* my grandfather. But Papa was stubborn; he out-bid the other fellow.

It was always at this point in the story-brushing that my grandmother would laugh. "I wasn't much of a cook back then," she would say (although she became a wonderful cook). "I know that lunch wasn't *that* good, but your grandfather made a big 'to-do' over it."

The other story tells of the simple, but profound, values of my grandparents. In those days a couple never even kissed until *after* they were married. Nanny told of the time when she and Papa stole a kiss on the front porch one evening just after they had become engaged. Evidently one of her brothers saw this. Later, in Nanny's presence, he exclaimed to another brother how he had heard of a couple who had kissed before they were married. He went on and on about how awful it was, making my grandmother, of course, feel terrible about the whole thing.

I always felt that, while I was brushing Nanny's hair, I was the most special person on earth. Much later, my sister and my cousin shared that they had been story-brushers also. Nanny always had a way of making *all* of her grandchildren feel special.

Nanny passed away just a few months before my first child was born. But I was able to pay her the ultimate compliment.

I named my daughter after her.

Bobbie Richardson Sutton is the office manager for Friendly Oaks Publications in Pleasanton, Texas, the publisher of *GRAND-Stories*.

91

Thanks for the Lesson, Grandpa

by Susan Luke

Grandpa lived most of his life in the Midwest; he raised his family there. As he grew older, the cold, harsh winters of that area were not kind to him and his arthritis. So he and Grandma sold their farm, he retired from his job, and they moved to the warmth of Arizona.

I was thrilled with the move. We lived in California, so it was easier for me to spend time with these two very special people.

From my earliest memories, Grandpa and I had a special relationship. It was Grandpa who taught me how to milk the goats on the farm and how to collect the eggs from the chicken house. Once he even let me name a new calf. She was all red with a tiny white star on her forehead; I named her Buttercup.

Grandpa would hold me in his lap for hours. Sometimes he would take out his dentures and playfully chew around my ears. I laughed and giggled—I loved it. While we sat together Grandpa would whisper wonderful stories in my ear. He always had a treat for me hidden in a pocket.

He never spoke harshly to anyone. Grandpa was a quiet man with a ready smile. And, as I recall, he always wore an old-fashioned, tweed-colored, golf cap.

Grandpa hated to be away from home; he preferred familiar surroundings. He would drive all day and all night to come and visit us, spending just one night, maybe two. Then he would drive straight back home. That's the way he was.

He believed in me, and was always my champion. He thought I was the "perfect" little girl. When I was very small, he and Grandma came for a visit. I remember my mother showing them the church where my daddy was the minister. She explained the different rooms and how they were used.

When we got to the furnace room, I said, "And this is the 'spanking room.'"

Silence. All I remember about the remainder of the 'tour' was the look of horror on Grandpa's face.

"You mean you *spank* this child?" he questioned my mother. My hero.

Toward the close of his life, Grandpa had difficulty just getting around. He would sit on the front porch with his pants legs rolled up above his knees. He would rub liniment on his sore knees and let them 'bake" in the sun; he insisted that it made him feel better.

By that time I was a teenager, I was looking to move on to more exciting things than sitting with Grandpa on the porch. I loved him, but I somehow felt that there would always be time to be with him—that he would *always* be there.

I was wrong.

It is important that we find the time to sit on the Porch of Life, a place where we can just think things through before we go charging off in yet another direction, quest, or adventure. It's important to take time to reflect and renew as we bring a rainbow of color to our awareness, especially as we share that awareness with those around us. We can learn a great deal from the examples of love given us in our childhood by those who are older and wiser.

Thanks for a valuable lesson, Grandpa. And thanks for being there for me. I love you.

Susan Luke is an international speaker, trainer, and author. She is president of The Luke Group and past-president of the Hawaii Chapter of the National Speakers Association. Susan is author of *Log Cabin Logic* (Luke Communications Group, 1995).

92

My Gramps

By Bob Perks

I love my Gramps. Notice that I still use the present tense, even though he died years ago. He had such an impact on my life that he continues to be a part of me still.

I can't picture Gramps without a perpetual smile. He always had a joke to tell, a song to sing, or a story with a punch line that I didn't always quite get. Nothing dirty, mind you, but lines like: "Did I ever tell you the story about when Moses tied his ass to a tree and walked 20 miles?"

"No, tell me," I'd say. Gramps would just laugh.

When he stayed for dinner, he would pick up the newspaper and look for "the list of people who don't have to pay taxes anymore." Whenever he left I would run to the paper and look for the list; I never found it. Years later I discovered the list—the obituaries.

The year he bought me a toy ukulele was the best. After dinner I would beg him to sing my favorite song, *The Three Little Fishes.* He would strum my ukulele with delight. Although he never hit the right  notes, it always sounded like heaven to me.

One of my fondest memories is of the Christmas when I met the *real* Santa Claus. My folks had told me they had located the real Santa at a local department store; and that they would take me there the Saturday before Christmas.

I was excited—and nervous.

"How do you know he's the *real* Santa?" I questioned.

"Well, test him," Mom suggested. "Ask him any question about yourself or our family. If he's the real Santa, he'll have the right answers."

And that's exactly what I did. Before I even sat on his lap, I asked him to name my favorite song. He knew it! He even sang it—just like Gramps.

He was the picture-perfect Santa; no padding needed. Under the red cap I could see *real* white hair. Tucked away in a very safe place I have a photograph of us together that night, me and the real Santa—me and Gramps.

There were not many sad moments between us, but I do remember one especially. I had grown up; Gramps had grown old. One night they rushed him to a hospital. He was in intensive care, so my visits with him were short. Sometimes the nurses would look the other way and give us a little extra time together.

During my last visit with Gramps we laughed a lot. I told him I had to leave, and he suddenly seemed confused (perhaps due to his weakened condition, the unfamiliar surroundings, interference from old memories and the medications he was taking). "Some friend you are—leaving me sitting on the curb," he said.

Now *I* was confused. He seemed angry, but I kissed him on his bald head, as I always did, and told him that I loved him. I turned to look back at him just before I closed the door, and once again I saw his incredible smiling face lit up like the Gramps I knew.

I had a decision to make as I left his hospital room that night. The next evening there was to be a Friday night dance for teens. I struggled with a decision I had to make—to go to the dance or visit Gramps. I went to the dance.

That night I had a wonderful time with my friends. I also enjoyed a few slow dances with potential girlfriends. We received a call from the hospital after I got home from the dance. Gramps had died. Some friend I turned out to be.

I *had* left him sitting on the curb.

I visit his grave periodically; it's down the road from my favorite aunt and uncle, and up the hill from Mom and Dad. I try not to dwell on sad memories; it hurts. But when I think of Gramps and the way he was, I am often surprised, and even overwhelmed, by the smiles those thoughts bring.

Like the thought of Moses and the tree.

Bob Perks is a professional speaker and the author of *The Flight of a Lifetime!* (Sparrow Distribution, 1997). He can be reached at (570) 696-2581. www.bobperks.com

93

A Gift of Joy

by Terry Paulson

Some people make jokes about their in-laws or that one weird relative from Burbank. But I am hard-pressed to compete with any of them in that category. I have been blessed beyond measure with a family rich in character, faith, and joy.

Both of my parents came from Swedish-American roots in the heartland of Illinois farm country. They remember paying a dime to watch movies projected on the wall of the Kirkland drugstore. My dad was on every sports team, not because he was a super athlete, but because they needed every boy in school to play or they couldn't field a team.

In Kirkland, there would be more people at the Fourth of July parade than there were people living in the town. The Lutheran church was the gathering place for the community. Their annual Confirmation pictures captured the rich mosaic of my family tree, a record that, even now, draws me to the church every time I visit. With such a rich family legacy, it might seem hard to select one relative who stands out. Ah, but then few had the privilege of knowing Vera Paulson, my grandma. Those who did know her never forgot her sparkling eyes and joyous nature.

You see, to a young child my Grandma Vera was more than just a grandma; she was hugs, laughter, stories, gingersnap cookies, and a joyous faith all wrapped up in one special person. Even though there were many grandchildren, and each of us could have competed for her attention, Grandma Vera made us all feel special—for in her eyes we were.

I especially treasured the times we had alone. I was ticklish as a child, but the warm, strong hands of my grandmother would give one great Swedish massage. While her fingers worked magic on my body, she'd tell stories about our Swedish ancestor, Putta Torpa Herr, a giant of a man who was over 7 feet tall, and whose gentle soul and helping nature was known throughout southern Sweden.

Grandma Vera also told me stories about her husband Fred, who had died suddenly before I was even 1-year-old. She talked about how he loved to sing and laugh. She said that, while many others just did their work, folks from all around could hear Fred singing hymns at the top of his voice while plowing the fields. The boys would hear laughter from the barn and think Fred was with a neighbor. But, as they would go in, expecting to find their father in conversation, they would find him laughing all to himself.

Grandma Vera would laugh as she told these stories. She was giving us a message about life: Life is a gift to be celebrated *every* day, no matter what happens. She lived that joy every day, and it showed in everything she did.

She talked about faith in God and His comforting presence that had come to her in times of struggle. She could quote scripture with ease and with a power that impressed me even as a young child.

I once asked her, "How do you remember all of those verses?" She replied with a knowing smile, "Terry, I hope you keep this close to your heart: If you read something often enough, no one can ever take it away from you." That message, and the grandmother who gave it, remain *very* close to my heart.

My Grandma Vera died on my birthday. Not a year of my life goes by without my remembering her as one of the greatest gifts God ever gave me. I had a wonderful opportunity to experience the sparkling eyes, the warm comforting hands, and the joy-filled faith of a grandmother I will never forget. My abiding hope is that someday my grandchildren will be able to say that I had even half the impact on them that Vera had on me.

May they know me as I knew her.

Terry Paulson, PhD, CSP, CPAE, from Agoura Hills, CA, is a psychologist who speaks and trains on the topic of change. He is a past-president of the National Speakers Association.

94

Use What You Have

by Glenn Van Ekeren

My grandparents played in a musical group that traveled and performed at various nursing homes, churches, and even the South Dakota State Fair. They were in their 80s and were still entertaining people on a weekly basis. No one in the band had any formal musical training. The group used a combination of instruments: piano, harmonica, accordion, musical saw, violin, and harpsichord. Their music drew repeated applause everywhere. The band was popular—and they were good. Their repeat bookings would have been the envy of any good agent.

One night over dinner, my grandparents were reflecting on their performances over the previous month. I was amazed at the number of miles they had traveled and the variety of people for whom they had performed.

I was curious and asked them why they continued to maintain such a rigorous schedule of travel and performances. "Oh," my over-80-year-old grandmother exclaimed, "those *old* people just love this stuff."

I learned some marvelous lessons from my grandparents. They taught me to never get caught up in the "If only ..." game, or the "Someday I'll ..." promise or explanation. I don't recall my grandparents wasting time on explaining why they couldn't or didn't do certain things. They didn't lament over the fact that they had no formal musical training. They didn't complain about getting older and finding it more difficult to travel, nor did they comment how their aging fingers and other body parts made it increasingly difficult to perform. They just went along doing the things they loved to do, using what they had to do it with. They always did it to the best of their ability and felt good about themselves in the process.

My grandparents remain my role models.

Glenn Van Ekeren is a professional speaker and the author of several books, including *The Speaker's Sourcebook* and *The Speaker's Sourcebook II* (Prentice-Hall, 1988, 1993). He now lives in Omaha, Nebraska.

95

He Counted Cars

by Lou Heckler

When I was still in grammar school, a significant event occurred in the life of my family. We lived a very rural existence, peaceful, quiet, and fairly uneventful, on property owned by my grandfather. However, a change was in store for all of us.

The Commonwealth of Pennsylvania approached my grandfather and informed him that a corner of his property lay in the right-of-way of a new highway that would run from Pittsburgh to the airport. We were right on the corridor. And, even though we were just 5 miles from downtown Pittsburgh, we had always felt as if we lived in the country. The cars that traveled our street on a given day could be counted on one hand.

After the new highway was in place, my grandfather would sit on his front porch, dressed in his camel-colored jacket and gray hat. He'd count the cars as they passed. He was continually amazed at the increase in traffic this road brought past our property. He used one of those little silver-colored counters. He clicked it once for each car that passed by the house.

He did it *every* day.

Each afternoon as I walked home from school, I'd stop and ask him how many cars he had totaled that day. He would look down at his counter and give me the number. It was a small moment, but a moment I cherish in my memory.

You see, small talk did not come easy for my grandfather. Conversation was somewhat difficult, and this exchange about the number of cars gave us a sweet starting point.

Sometimes a beginning, a starting point, is all we need.

My grandfather died when I was 12 years old. I can still see him clearly, however, sitting on the porch counting cars, and shaking his head in amazement.

Low Heckler, CSP, CPAE is a motivational humorist and trainer.

96

Mavis
by Kay Todd

I was waiting to register at this "mom and pop" motel on the Olympic Peninsula. She really looked out of place working behind the check-in counter. I'm not certain if it was her perfect manicure, her obviously expensive clothes, or her articulate manner that captured my attention. I just knew I was intrigued, and that I wanted to learn more about her.

Her name was Mavis.

I checked into my room, then went out for a walk. While roaming the grounds, I happened upon her. Mavis was sitting out back of the motel enjoying a cigarette and a cup of coffee. She was captivated by the antics of an otter playing in the water.

Moving over to where she was sitting, I took a seat next to her. "So, how's everything going," I asked. "How do you like working at a motel?"

"Oh, everything's just great," she replied. "But I don't just work here; I *live* here." She said it with a certain pride in her voice.

A long moment passed, then she continued. "I have a house up there on the bluff." She pointed off into the distance. "See; it's that white Victorian with the veranda and a great view of the Sound." She paused again. "But I'm not living there right now."

"My son, Jonah, his wife, and my grandchildren are living there. When Jonah and my daughter-in-law decided to enter graduate school full-time, they both resigned their jobs and sold their home. That way, they could afford the tuition and have enough to rent an apartment in the city closer to the university."

"I saw in their situation the perfect opportunity for me to give a gift that only this grandmother could give. I gave them my house for 2 years."

Mavis was smiling. "My grandchildren can stay in their school, with their friends, and in safe and familiar surroundings. They won't have to live in the crowded city surrounded by strangers."

I was speechless.

She continued. "Even more importantly, the children come here to the motel to be with me every day after school. They can stay here until their mom and dad get home. I believe it's important for children to know their grandparents; don't you?"

I nodded in agreement.

"Anyway," she declared, "I was pretty bored with my life and my corporate career. I had been going into the city every day for 22 years. I was ready for something new, an adventure. So, I took this job so that I could have my adventure and be with my grandchildren all at the same time!"

She slipped into thought for a moment, then shared: "Life is not about where you live, you know. It's about who you *are*."

She's right, you know. Above everything else, life *is* about who we are. Mavis, the grandmother, is giving her family the unselfish gifts of time, love, and a home —gifts only she can give. And her actions are an encouragement, a lesson to others.

Here's a "Thank You" to all the generous and thoughtful grandparents in the world, and a special "Thanks" to you, Mavis.

Kay Todd is a professional speaker and teacher. She speaks on the subject of sales excellence, and is based in both Scottsdale, Arizona, and Cincinnati, Ohio.

97

Memories

by Lowell Streiker

My paternal grandfather, Morris Streiker, died when I was about 3 years old. Regretfully, I have no memories of him. So, to me, the word "grandfather" means Meyer Peller, my maternal grandfather.

Grandfather Peller was a wiry little man who had immigrated from East Prussia to Chicago at the time of the 1892 Colombian Exposition. When he was only a teenager, his father set a peddler's pack of matches on his back and sent him out to make his own way. Some years later he married my grandmother, Julia Saunders, a beautiful fellow immigrant from the Baltic, and still a teenager. My mother was their fifth child and their first daughter. I was my parents' first child, my grandparents' first grandchild.

My mother's folks lived, for most of their lives, in a small, frame house in Maywood, Illinois, about 20 miles west of the Chicago Loop. They were wretchedly poor by today's standards. Grandpa delivered Ole Colony Ginger Ale and Orange Crush to small "mom and pop" grocery stores and private homes in his ancient Model A Ford truck. For many years he raised corn, tomatoes, green beans, cucumbers, onions, and endive on an empty lot across the street from his home.

Grandpa wore wool slacks and jackets from a collection of out-of-style suits. Grandma had a few housecoats and only one or two nice dresses. Everything they owned seemed old, rusted, and musty. To the eyes of this child, however, it all seemed magical.

I delighted in walking to the market with Grandpa to buy poultry and egg noodles for Grandma's chicken soup. She made it in a big kettle on the stove, a kettle that seemed to be inexhaustible — bottomless.

Being with my grandfather always gave me an incomparable sense of security. Everyone we met seemed to know Grandpa, and I was instantly recognized as his grandson. I would be complimented by strangers (to me) who would tell me how much I reminded them of my mother's brothers (many of them had gone to high school with my uncles). Some would say "He looks like Leo," while others would say, "No, he looks more like Phil—*before* he broke his nose." Grandpa would simply insist, "Label (Lowell) looks just like himself."

I will never forget the odors of their old place: the fragrance of Grandma's challah (egg bread), all the delicious smells of meals eaten and enjoyed, and the acrid pungency of the leftovers that were thrown to the wild cats who lived nowhere, but everywhere. That old house was my amusement park, refuge, retreat, and sanctuary all rolled into one. It's been demolished, torn down now for many years, yet it's *still* my legacy. Its memory will be mine for as long as I live.

I spent my summers, school holidays, and many other times with them in that barely livable old house. The furniture and rugs in that house were all dank, dark, and woolly. That house needed my grandfather's constant attention—just to keep it from collapsing.

One day, when he was a very old man, Grandpa fell from the roof while making repairs; he broke several ribs. Soon, though, he was up and back on the roof. He and the old house were a mutually dependent ecosystem. Neither would have survived long without the other.

Their mostly Black neighborhood (where they had lived, without incident, for over 40 years) grew tense in the 1960s. When a brick was thrown through their front window, they decided to move. They sold that beloved place to the housing authority, and the old house was bulldozed to the ground. I always considered that demolition a wasted effort because, without Grandpa's constant attention, it would have tumbled down in a few months anyway. Today a single elm tree stands there as a witness to the lives and memories that resided there.

My grandparents moved to a comfortable apartment on the south side of Chicago. Without his house and his truck, and with his vision failing, Grandpa was reduced to watching a fading old black and white TV that his children had given him years before. He simply awaited death, it seemed, hoping his children and grandchildren would visit him once in awhile.

I was in graduate school when Grandpa suffered a massive heart attack; he was not expected to live long. I sent him a letter telling him about my answers to my son's questions regarding what I did when I was his age. I told Grandpa that I would tell him about the time I spent with him, and about the time I helped him plant his garden. (Grandpa couldn't figure out why the onions I planted took so long to grow. When he finally harvested them, Grandpa said they were the *longest* onions he had ever seen. I had planted all the bulbs upside-down!)

I was told that his spirits lifted when that letter was read to him; the dear old man actually rallied.

I last saw him in 1964; he was 85 and I was 25. There had been some tension between us because of my conversion to Christianity. On this occasion my grandfather, grandmother, and I sat at their kitchen table and talked it over until we were, once again, comfortable with one another. Grandpa told me he had read some of my articles that had been published in religious journals (I had given copies to my parents, and they had passed them on to him). We discussed the content of the articles, especially the notion that the essence of religion is not how one prefers to practice their beliefs as much as how they respond to the needs of fellow human beings. During that conversation Grandpa told me that he felt I was a "real Jew." He pointed to his heart as he said it, saying it first in Yiddish, then English. Then he added, "I am *very* proud of you."

A few weeks later he died of another heart attack.

Several years later I wrote my first book, *The Promise of Buber*. I dedicated it to my grandparents. I gave an inscribed copy to Grandma, although she never learned to read or write English. I had not known, until she told me, that Martin Buber was one of my grandfather's favorite writers, and that he had often read Buber's books in Yiddish.

I remember, and I reminisce. When my grandparents lived in Maywood, I would visit them whenever I felt the need. There is no balm to the spirit that measures up to the look on the face of someone who loves you simply because you exist. I always kept a Bluebird bus token on my keychain so I could get to their house. After my visit, when I was ready to leave, they would always give me two more tokens.

I kept the last token on my keychain until my Grandma's death in 1973.

Lowell D. Streiker, PhD, is an inspirational humorist as well as a serious phenomenologist of religion who has written, co-authored, edited, and contributed to more than 20 books. Lowell is a father, stepfather, and grandfather who lives with his wife, Connie, in Cottonwood, California.

98

My Grandfather Taught Me a Lesson About Procrastination

by Cher Holton

Sometimes we just have to learn things the hard way. That's how I internalized a real life lesson about procrastination. May this story encourage you and others to "do it now." When it comes to telling others that you love them, don't wait. You could be too late.

I have always enjoyed making cards for friends and family. But I wasn't very good at getting them off in the mail on time. Typically I procrastinated until the event the card was celebrating was past. But, figuring it was better late than never, I would still send it out.

My grandfather was one of my greatest fans; he loved anything I ever made. He always took care to keep it, make a big fuss over it, and then shared it with others.

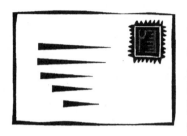

I especially remember the year I thought I'd be real smart and make a card for my grandfather that was *designed* to be sent late. The card had a verse about being late and having another day to celebrate. I mailed it the day of his birthday.

That very night we got a call telling us that my grandfather had suddenly died. I'll never forget arriving for his funeral the same day my card arrived. If I had just sent it on time, he would have seen it and would have been reminded, one more time, how much I loved him.

Cher Holton, PhD, is a corporate impact consultant focusing on Bringing Harmony to Life with customers, team members, and yourself. She is a Certified Speaking Professional and a Certified Meeting Consultant.

99

A Special Treat

by Jeff Davidson

When my grandfather read the daily newspaper, it was his habit to always sit in his special reclining chair in the den. He seemed to always have ample coins in his pockets—his *baggy* pants pockets. When he finished the newspaper and left the room, we grandchildren made a beeline for the chair. We knew, from experience, that there was a good chance we might find some coins down in the recesses of his chair. We almost always found some.

We harvested coins from his chair for years.

Maybe our grandfather knew he was making those little donations to his grandkids, but he never let us know he knew. Certainly no one ever got rich from the coins we found. But it was something we all looked forward to, one of the many special treats we experienced when we visited grandma and grandpa's house.

Jeff Davidson offers simple advice that makes profound differences in people's lives. He is a keynote speaker and author. Visit www.BreathingSpace.com for a list of books and tapes.

100

Gram's Wooden Spoon

by Ernie Wendell

When I was a boy growing up in Chicago, my mother worked outside our home. Mom was the exception to the norm of women of her day. I cannot remember a time when she didn't have a job. Because she was a working mom, my grandmother was the designated "honcho" of the kids in our family.

Gram, as we called her, was very keen on President Teddy Roosevelt's image of American leadership; she spoke softly, and she carried a big stick.

Gram ran a no-nonsense, taut, and tight ship, and she actually carried (at least from my perspective) a *very* big stick. Only Gram's stick was a gigantic wooden spoon—a character-building instrument of the first order! She *always* had that spoon in her hand. It was her badge of authority.

I thought she even slept with that darned spoon! I always felt a little sorry for my grandfather, lying in bed with a wooden spoon.

Gram used that oaken stick like a writer uses exclamation marks. Whenever she wanted to make a point, she would lift that spoon up in the air, wave it around in a menacing sort of way, then point it at one of us kids. If the designated "doer" didn't move quickly enough to suit her, the spoon would make its move.

For maximum effect (and minimal damage), the spoon was usually aimed toward the lower posterior. However, I was so quick and successful at avoiding the spoon that Gram changed her tactics with me. She would simply reach out and quickly pop me right on top of the head. I got popped on the head so many times, I think it killed the roots of my hair, causing my early baldness. The thing I remember most was that it hurt, and we tried to avoid it.

It must have been effective; we seldom disobeyed Gram more than once.

Some folks might think that my grandmother was too tough on us kids. Her actions may even seem harsh by today's loose standards. I believe she did the best she could—which is all we can ever ask of anyone. We loved her totally, in spite of her spoon. Yes, we learned discipline by way of Gram's wooden spoon. I have never forgotten the lessons. Today, whenever I get sluggish in pursuit of my goals, or lazy in meeting my objectives, I mentally (just mentally, mind you) pop myself on the head with Gram's wooden spoon. It works every time!

Do you have a wooden spoon in your life? Could you use one?

Ernie Wendell is the compiler/editor of *GRAND-Stories*. This story is reprinted from his first book, *Stepping Stones to Success*. It is used here with the permission of Ernie Wendell and Milestone Publications (1997).

101

Taste Time

by Jose Stevens

In the early 1950s, when I was very young (perhaps 4 or 5 years of age), I loved to spend as much time as I could with my Mexican grandmother. Nana, as I called her, was a short, stout woman with dark wrinkles covering her weathered face. But her merry eyes were bright and ageless.

Nana was already in her 80s, and she showed her toothless gums whenever she would throw her head back and laugh with complete abandonment—which was often. She spoke only Spanish.

At the time, we were living in an old farmhouse in East Hollywood. It was, I believe, the original family place, built before the orchards were cut down and the neighborhoods appeared. I remember it as a good place to live, and a good time to live there.

I had this favorite homemade candy, my grandmother's specialty. I would spend hours helping her make this special treat. Nana called it "cajeta," a kind of thick syrup made by cooking milk and sugar.

Nana would start the candy ritual by scouring the inside of the great copper pot (which she had brought with her from Mexico) with a slice of lemon. When the pot was ready, she would pour in the ingredients. Then the pot and contents were placed over a low, blue flame.

My job was to stir the pot. I'd stir for hours with a long, wooden spoon. I would ask Nana, over and over, if the candy was ready.

It was hard to wait. As the ingredients slowly boiled down, the syrup grew thicker and thicker. The air filled with a delicious aroma.

"Is it ready yet?" I would ask her in Spanish.

"No," Nana would reply, shaking her head. She would say it over and over until the moment arrived when she would finally announce that the cajeta was ready. She would scoop it into a bowl and let it sit to cool.

Waiting for the candy to cool was the toughest wait of all. More than once I'd burn my fingers trying to sample the still hot cajeta while Nana's back was turned. Compassionately she would dry my tears and let me lick the spoon.

Now that was really living!

Jose Luis Stevens, PhD, is a business consultant, counselor, international lecturer and author of eight books. A member of the National Speakers Association, he makes his home in Santa Fe, New Mexico.

102

Time with Grandpa

by Kathy Zullo

Some of the moments I remember most with my Grandpa Clyde are the simplest ones. One time when I was 5, visiting his farm, he took me for a ride in his truck as we went to town to visit the combine repair shop. He gave me a nickel for the Coke machine (the kind where the green bottle slid down the chute when you turned the handle). As the welder fixed the broken combine part, I sat quietly and drank my Coke (which Mom would *never* let me have.)

Now, a moment like this might not seem like much, but it has certainly stayed with me through the years. I think it has such significance to me because it was the first time that Grandpa and I had spent together.

We did lots of things together after that. We would walk the fields and he would show me how corn reproduces, and he would point out the differences between a male and female melon blossom. He taught me how to bait a hook with a big, juicy earthworm to catch bass in his lake.

When I was 13, Grandpa let me drive his truck around the barnyard. And he didn't even mind when the truck's old transmission cried out in protest to my poor attempts at shifting gears.

Thinking back, what mattered the most to me was that I spent time with him individually—not with my sister or brothers. I also spent a lot of quality one-on-one time with my Grandma Lang. My grandparents thought I (as well as each one of their other 25 grandchildren) was special, and showed it.

Those were the happiest days of my childhood.

Reprinted from the book, *The Nanas and the Papas (A Boomer's Guide to Grandparenting)*, by Kathryn and Allan Zullo. Used with permission of The Wordsellers, Inc. and Andrews McMeel Publishing (1998)

103

The Book of Life

by Michael A. Aun

Our family is of Lebanese decent; both sides of the house hail from Beirut. My grandfather's name was Eli Mack. Well, not really; you see, his *real* name was Elias Skaff. However, like so many who came through immigration at the turn of the century, the immigration officer could not pronounce his name. My grandfather was told, "Look, Mac, you need to change that name." So he did; he took the name "Mack."

Eli Mack was eventually elected mayor of Lexington, South Carolina. He held the office for a number of years before it was discovered that, at least technically, he was still an illegal alien. He had never completed the requirements, nor had he officially taken the oath of citizenship. So, some time after he had been elected mayor, he took the necessary steps to become an American citizen.

Everything in its own time.

He was my maternal grandfather. I called him "Jidu" (pronounced "Jiddy"), which, translated from Arabic, means "grandfather." He called me his "Hyetti," which roughly translates to "the breath of my life," or "my heart." He would say to me, "Hyetti, God blesses the man who gives advice; but he blesses a thousand times more the man who takes the advice and uses it." I have never forgotten that.

He was my mentor; I was so fortunate. When I was 11, he handed me a blank book, saying, "Hyetti, here is a gift for you."

"But Jiddy," I replied in surprise, "there is nothing in this book. It has no value."

"What you write in the book will make it valuable, Hyetti."

As soon as I had the blank book, my grandfather instructed me to sit down and write in it 500 things I wanted to do in my life.

Hey, I'm only 11; I don't even know 500 things! So I leaned on Jiddy's wisdom. He said, "Watch the television, read the newspaper, and pay attention to the people around you. Then make your list."

I did, and I did.

That list has grown substantially; today it contains thousands of things. Did I accomplish everything on that original list of 500? Of course not. But I have accomplished, or have crossed off what could not be accomplished, to a total of 478 items.

I have checked off the majority of the list as being completed; I've done those things. Which ones did I scratch? Well, I have concluded that I am not going to be governor of the state. But I most likely would not have stood for election to the House of Representatives if I hadn't had "governor" on my list.

I also know I'm not going to be a priest, and I'm not going to be President of the United States. I'm never going to climb Mount Everest, either. However, many of the skills I possess today came through those original goals and what it took to achieve them—goals set by an 11-year-old. Thank, you, Jiddy.

I started with that one journal; I now have over 200. I routinely take notes at meetings, in church, and during down times at my kids' wrestling matches or choir practice. I turn waiting time into writing time. Thank you, Jiddy.

I now realize that the greatest single benefit that I received from the one who called me his heart is the legacy I can now leave to my three boys. It is something they will have long after I am gone. Yes, to my wife and my sons, by way of my grandfather, I give the gift of a profound and lasting love.

Again, thank you, Jiddy.

Michael A. Aun, FIC, LTUTCF, CSP, is a keynote speaker, author of four books, syndicated columnist and a businessman. He is the 1978 winner of the World Championship of Public Speaking. www.aunline.com

104

Reward System

by Ernie Wendell

My grandfather, Frank Mueller, immigrated to this country from Germany at the turn of the century. He was highly skilled, a master baker. He made his way to the city of Chicago, where a job had been promised.

As I remember the story, my grandfather worked as an employed baker for several years, never earning more than $14.00 a week. (Today it is very difficult to imagine someone working for that amount of money.) Somehow, with that small salary, he was not only able to survive, but he also managed to marry and set up housekeeping with my grandmother (Amanda), start a family, and still save enough of his weekly income to go into business for himself. He prospered. My earliest recollection is of living over the bakery and behind the store.

Three children were born to Frank and Amanda; two survived, my mother Eleanor and her brother Hans. Although my grandfather lost almost everything he owned in the bank crash of the early 30s, he was able to hold on to some property—two buildings on Elston Avenue. One housed the bakery, a behind-the-store apartment and a second-story flat. The other building included a storefront and a second- and third-story flat.

The family endured the Great Depression on the baking skills of my grandfather. His bread was an absolute delight and defies description, impossible to match in taste and texture. He sold retail out of the storefront and wholesale to other neighborhood bakeries out of the back.

My grandfather was a first-rate sneezer, one who must sneeze often and robustly (he sneezed up a storm in sound and fury). He always sneezed into one of those giant-sized colorful red and blue bandanas. He made certain all of us kids understood that a sneeze should never, ever, under *any* circumstances, be stifled. We were told that, when you felt a sneeze coming on, you should turn your back on anyone present, put your head back and let it rip! This technique was an absolute necessity for my grandfather. If he had ever put his hand over his mouth when he sneezed, I'm afraid he could well have blown apart.

By the time I was 7 or 8 years old, it was my job to take his beer pail down to the corner saloon once each day to get it filled. It was extremely hot work in the bakery; a little cool beer really helped. My grandfather also made his own wine; a common practice in those times. The wine, however, had to be kept away from my grandmother because she really objected to the drinking of alcohol. (However, she did tolerate that one small pail of beer each day. She didn't like it; she just made it a practice to look the other way.)

In those days of wood-fired ovens, baking required lots of long hours, very difficult work and iron-hard men. An occasional glass of wine and a daily pail of beer was my grandfather's reward system.

It worked for him.

Ernest J. Wendell is the compiler of *GRAND-Stories*. Ernie is an inspirational speaker and seminar leader. He is the author of the book, *Stepping Stones to Success* (Milestone Publications, 1997).

105

Real Wealth

by C. Roy Hunter

I'm proud that C. Roy Hunter was my grandfather. His mother was an Indian woman and his father was a hobo. My grandfather had to drop out of school in the 7th grade to go to work to support his father.

Adversity can make you or break you.

Grandfather developed a very special interest in photography, something that became much more than just a hobby. It helped him find his true path that eventually took him from rags to riches. He became a cinematography pioneer in Hollywood during the golden era of the early movies. My grandfather worked on such classics as the silent screen versions of *Phantom of the Opera, All's Quiet on the Western Front*, and the first *Dracula* and *Frankenstein* movies. Numbered among his personal friends were Cecil B. DeMille and Walt Disney (whom I met when I was a child).

But good fortune did not go to my grandfather's head. He had learned from hard experience what it meant to be poor. When I was only 6 years old he taught me a very valuable lesson about money; he handed me a $100 dollar-bill (worth a lot more in 1949 than it is today).

I remember that incident vividly. As I looked at that $100 dollar-bill in my hand I exclaimed, "Wow, that's a *lot* of money."

My grandfather measured his words and spoke carefully. "Always remember, son, that money is only a tool, a tool that can be put to use in pursuit of good or bad; it has no lasting value."

He continued. "Do remember that you cannot take money with you when your life is finished. The lasting values of life are found in things such as love, honesty, and character. Use money wisely, because you will not be judged by how much money you have, but by how well you use it."

Grandfather's words of wisdom have remained with me during all the years of my life, including the lean years of struggle, the good years of plenty, and all the years in between.

I often think about what he said with a certain hope that those who are fortunate, and who have been graced with plenty, will awaken to the realization that there are those who are less fortunate financially, but who enjoy the richness of a life of love. Others might be secure financially but are bankrupt in their ability to demonstrate any compassion at all.

Real wealth comes from loving and being loved.

My grandfather challenged me with this question: "If you were to wake up some morning and find yourself in another dimension with only your consciousness to support you, will you be wealthy in the only way that *really* counts?"

Well, will you?

C. Roy Hunter is the published author of four books. He is a consultant and trainer.

106

Grandmother, I'm Here!

by Barbara D. Tooker

Taking a deep breath and preparing myself for what my parents had told me to expect, I walked into her room at the nursing home with a smile on my face and a bounce in my step. Exuding energy and health, I gaily said, "Grandma, I'm here."

"Oh, Barbara, I knew you'd come; So glad you're here," breathed my grandmother. Her voice was weak and hushed. I reached out, wrapped her in my arms, and whispered, "I came as soon as I could, Grandmother." It was then that my tears flowed silently and my throat constricted painfully; the words echoed back ... back ... back through time.

"Grandmother, I'm here!" I shouted through the back door screen.

"Oh, Barbara; so glad you're here." And, in the next moment she added, "Let's go gather the eggs. I need help with the settin' hens." Hand-in-hand we headed toward the hen house, she with her big pail and me with my little pail.

She was 41; I was 3. I loved being with her. I always got to set the table at Grandmother's house, a task I loved doing because of her bright, colorful Fiestaware. Sometimes I'd make sure I matched everything in the same color at a single place setting, and sometimes I'd be very artistic and mix all the colors together in a splash of perpetual spring.

"It'll be our rule," Grandmother would tell me, "that no one can be sad or mad when they sit down to eat at our table."

"Yep, it's our rule!" I'd chirp. "Besides, who can be sad or mad sitting at a table that looks like a field of flowers?" And so, all of my life I have smiled whenever I have had the good fortune to sit down with Fiestaware. This is part of the fabric of my life; for this I thank her.

As the years progressed, she taught me how to sew, crochet, bake, and make butter in the new electric churn. She taught me how to iron clothes using her new built-in ironing board that had a secret fold-up spot in the laundry room. I learned how to take care of African violets, and how to tell when the roast was done. We would can the whole garden crop. We plucked chicken feathers and dressed out the hen.

Grandmother taught me to respect my elders, to honor a good education, and to value honest work. She even taught me how to play Solitaire a million ways. She told me which behaviors she thought were right and which were wrong, but I never recall her telling me I was wrong.

She sympathized with me when my parents disciplined me. She would make comforting little clicking sounds when I'd tell her all the horrible things my parents wanted me to do (like clean up my room, help around the house, take care of my brothers and sisters—you know, things that couldn't possibly have been fair!). And so, I have smiled whenever my daughters wanted to run to my mother or my grandmother with the injustices I have heaped upon them from time to time. This, too, is part of the fabric of my life; for this I thank her.

Every fall, just like clockwork, my grandmother and grandfather would whisk me off to buy school clothes. This was always an eventful trip to a faraway place where we'd get to stay overnight. Oh, the luxury of it all: two pairs of shoes, five dresses, sometimes a winter coat, and brand new underwear. Then, of course, there were the new Big Chief tablets, pencils, an eraser, a pencil sharpener, and a lunch box. What a comfort to go off to school all decked out in the newest, latest fashions. (At least I knew I'd never bring dishonor to my family; no one would find me in raggedy underwear if a car or the school bus ever hit me!) This, too, is part of the fabric of my life; for this I thank her.

When my grandparents built their lovely new brick home, they also bought new furniture to go with it. "Out with the old; in with the new," was their motto. Newness was definitely one of their goals. Grandmother was so proud of everything in the new house, a house that she had designed and furnished.

To celebrate, we had the famous family meal at their new dining room table, which was covered with a homemade crocheted tablecloth and matching runners on the sideboard. The Fiestaware remained in the cupboard; the "good" dishes and silverware came out. "The Meal" was always turkey and dressing, mashed potatoes and gravy, cranberry salad, homemade rolls and butter, a huge relish tray with plenty of black olives, real milk straight from the cow—and pumpkin pie. And so, all of my life I have smiled when I, too, use the handmade crocheted tablecloth and the matching runners when *I* now create "The Meal." Another part of the fabric of my life; for this I thank her.

When our oldest daughter, Michelle, was 2 years old, we made a visit to my grandparents. Just as we were getting out of the car, I said to Michelle, "Now run to the door and say, 'Grandmother, I'm here!'" And she did.

Back came the reply, "Oh, Michelle! So glad you're here."

I knew then that my daughter would find the same kind of comfort in this great-grandmother that I had found in the grandmother. And it was no different when Becky came along 2-and-a-half years later.

When we would prepare to leave, I'd always look for things to put away, the children's messes to clean up. One day I got out the glass cleaner to wipe the fingerprints off her glass door.

Grandmother stopped me. "Oh, please don't take away the fingerprints. That's all I have left when they go; I want the memories." I know that some day, when Michelle and Becky bring their children for a visit with me, I will smile, and I too will insist on keeping the fingerprints. This is part of the fabric of my life; for this I thank her.

I never smell lilacs or peonies without Grandmother's memories rushing back to me. I never see little ceramic pixies in a shop without memories recurring. I never see handmade crochet work, wrap up in an afghan, attend church suppers or bazaars, fix a chicken casserole, or bake cinnamon rolls without thinking of her. I never see Oddfellows and Rebekah's Lodge signs, play a game of Bridge, or use White Shoulders perfume without my grandmother coming to mind. There's not a room in my house that doesn't contain something Grandmother had made. I enjoy those memories every day. I have this richly woven fabric of my life that smells, feels, looks, and tastes like Grandmother's things. They comfort me; they help me accept the onward march of the generations. For this I thank her.

These are the memories that come flooding back to me in the nursing home as I gently hold her in my arms. Now, a month later, I further understand why the unstoppable and sometimes unexpected tears stream down my face, and why my throat constricts when the memories well up; unbidden, but always welcome. Every Mother's Day, I honor my paternal grandmother. I pay her the tribute she deserves for being a responsible elder in both our family and our hometown community. Regardless of her faults and foibles (and she, like all of us, had them), she is the salt of the earth. She has listened and heard the drumbeat of time; she's a participant in the march of the generations. She has taught me to march well, to care for my family and my community.

Now my parents are about to take on the mantle of the elders. They will assume the responsibility and continue the march. They, too, have added strength and riches to the fabric of my life. They learned much from my grandmother, who learned from her parents and grandparents. The march of time.

Grandmother dearest, I wish I had the power to take away your Alzheimer's disease. I wish I had the power to reduce your confusion and ease your humiliation, but I don't know how. You are now in the hands of some far greater power whose plan for you remains a mystery. I wish for you, and for the part of you that has already gone, a safe journey. I do know what you will leave behind.

The most important part of all is that I have learned your lessons, have seen you in action, and have heard your words. I shall treasure them and care for them; I will share them with my daughters. When it is my turn, I will accept the mantel of the elders, for I, too, am a part of the interwoven march of the generations. Grandmother, may this day and everyday be peaceful, and may your memories sustain you and wrap you in love.

Grandmother, I'm here.

Barbara D. Tooker, author of *Accent on Parenting* (Affordable Educators, 2000), is a professional speaker and Executive Director of the National Parenting Institute. This story first appeared in "Country Review" magazine (May, 1994). www.barbtooker.com

107

Remembering Grandpa
by Tim Richardson

I stared at the picture of my grandfather, taken shortly before he died. He looked good wearing his favorite cap, sporting a mustache, and backdropped by the autumn colors of fall.

My thoughts drifted back to the day I took that picture. If I had known then that it was to be his last fall season, his last picture, the last day I would spend with my healthy grandfather—well, I would have spent it very differently. I would have asked him to, once again, tell me the stories of his childhood. I would have been happy to listen to his favorite jokes—just to hear him laugh. I'm sure I would have asked him to tell me about his days as a chaplain in World War II. I would have brought him some treats from Whitman's Bakery (the ones he loved so much). Maybe I would have taken him downtown for lunch. We would have enjoyed just being together, listening to his favorite music, and playing his favorite games.

If I'd had the opportunity on that last day, I would have thanked him most heartily for helping me through college, for lending me money to start my own business, and for accepting my wife as one of his grandchildren.

I would have thanked him for playing chess with me when I was a teenager, for listening to me dream dreams about my business. We could have taken a walk in the woods, and I would have asked him questions about plants and trees—just to hear the cadence in his voice and record it in my memory. I know I would have hugged him, and he would have known how much I loved him.

I loved my grandfather very much. He was absolutely the kindest, dearest, most loving man I ever knew. And that's not just *my* opinion. Everyone who knew my grandfather held him in high regard.

He had a special way of making people feel good. Certainly he had never been the president of some big corporation, or an Olympic athlete or even a celebrity. The small town of Waynesville will never name a street or a building after my grandfather; nor will the history books mention his name. Nonetheless, he was a great man.

My grandfather served his country, his community, and his family. He was a role model, an honest, hard-working man with great wisdom and the fortitude to live by the high standards he set. He believed completely in truthfulness and integrity. He bought automobiles made in America—and he bought U.S. Savings Bonds.

He encouraged entrepreneurship by making financial contributions and giving insightful advice to all his grandchildren. My life will be well-lived if I am remembered for being even half the man he was.

Today I am seated at his desk, the same desk that first belonged to his father. I hold another picture in my hand, a picture of my infant son, Russell. I offer a prayer. I pray that my son will be as positively influenced by me as I have been influenced by my grandfather. My son and my grandfather have a common bond—they share the same name.

Someday, when little Russell grows up, he will hear stories of his great-grandfather, the man who married and lived with my grandmother for 65 years. Russell will learn of the man my father knew for 64 years, and I knew for 32 years. And he'll learn to cherish this great man as we do.

Tim Richardson is a professional speaker and author of *Jump Starts: Wit and Wisdom to SUPERCHARGE Your Day* and *Letters from Daddy (New Dawn Press, 1998, 2000)*. (904) 249-0919. www.TimRichardson.com

108

Lessons from Gram
by Ernie Wendell

Gram was, to say the least, unusual. She was a great task master, and a living example of determination. For instance, she was a stickler for cleanliness. She scrubbed our kitchen floor every morning. Even when she grew older and was physically limited she called on my Aunt Trudy to continue the daily ritual.

I can still see that old galvanized bucket, that huge scrub brush, and that giant-sized, yellow-colored, ugly bar of Fels-Naptha soap. This happened to be the very same soap Gram used to wash out my mouth with whenever I said something nasty. (Having your mouth washed out with soap was a rather common cure for "nasty mouth" back in those days. However, only my grandmother used Fels-Naptha soap). Believe me, I can *still* taste it.

Gram was the reigning matriarch of the family (she controlled the purse strings). Everyone paid her homage. She had a few idiosyncrasies. Perhaps I should refer to them as "principles." For instance, no one, and I do mean *no one*, smoked in her presence. She did not consider it a clean habit.

The one exception I recall occurred when I came home on my first leave in the Navy. Not only did she break her rule about smoking in her presence, Gram actually gave me a small dish for my ashes, a wondrous compromise to cleanliness that I never expected. I suppose it was her way of saying, "Welcome home."

She was just as adamant about alcohol, but I never tried her on that issue. My grandfather, however, would make Dandelion wine, then hide the bottles in the woodpile (a large stack of cut logs to feed the wood-burning ovens in our bakery). He knew she would never go near that dirty pile of wood. His "stash" was safe.

Almost daily as I grew older, I would, along with Gram, draw the closing shift in our bakery store. We opened before dawn; we never closed before full dark. Those were long, long days. Every night the remaining bakery product was removed from the store to make room for tomorrow's fresh bake. Then the cleaning began. All the display cases and the long front display window had to be scrubbed spotless. I worked; Gram mostly supervised. It was a good arrangement—for her. She always made sure the job was done right. We never had a sanitary inspection that I was aware of, but we certainly never needed one.

When I first announced to Gram that I had joined the U.S. Navy, she responded in her rather typical fashion. She said, "Don't you know that the navy is filled with bummers?" She went on to explain that when she was a young girl in Germany, the judge would give the bad boys two choices: jail or the navy. "Yah," she remarked, "full of bummers. Don't be a bummer!" (She was wrong, you know. The navy I served didn't have many bummers.)

The one thing I had going for me was the U.S. Navy's reputation for cleanliness. Her opinion was that, in the navies of the world, there was more opportunity to be clean and stay clean. One thing for sure, my early training by Gram paid big dividends. No one had to teach this "swab jockey" how to keep things clean.

Reprinted from Ernie Wendell's *Stepping Stones to Success*, and used with permission from Milestone Publications (1997).

109

Put Your Best Foot Forward

by Jim Folks

Daddy Wade was my mother's stepdaddy; my grand-stepdaddy. He was a tinkerer who could fix anything. Every time Daddy Wade came to visit us, my mom would put him to work on any and every thing that was broken. He would immediately proceed to take care of business.

I loved to follow him around and watch him work. He was always methodical, calm, and effective. Before the first day of the visit was over, everything around the place would be in working order.

My brother and I spent our summers with our grandparents in Mississippi. Because both sets of our grandparents lived only a few miles apart, I was able to spend quite a lot of time with Daddy Wade. He was an early riser, always up before the sun. Whether he was visiting us, or if we were visiting him, I would get up just to be with him.

Daddy Wade was a quiet man with a very gentle spirit. I never heard him raise his voice or say an unkind word to or about anyone. There was something about him that just made me want to be with him. I don't have much recollection of what I used to talk to him about, but I always knew he wanted to hear what I had to say. He would just sit and listen and encourage me in such a special way that I felt very important and loved by the time he left to go to work.

Looking back, I can see how important the time I spent with Daddy Wade was for me. He gave me the gift of listening. He demonstrated to me the ability to be quiet and peaceful, regardless of what was going on. He was kind, generous with his talents, and always available to help others. His method of teaching was just to live it out in front of you. But there was one lesson that Daddy Wade taught me directly; it had to do with my shoes.

Growing up, I only had one pair of shoes. Sundays we were required to go to church. I remember throwing lots of fits about having to go to church, having to dress up, and especially about having to polish my shoes.

Daddy Wade was not a church-going man. (I can just picture him sitting quietly and having a wonderful, peaceful, holy experience while *we* were at church.) Early one morning, Daddy Wade and I were sitting and talking. I don't remember how the topic came up, but I do remember him saying to me, "You should always put your best foot forward, and, when you do, make sure your shoes are clean and shining."

That's the day my shoe shining fits stopped. To this day, keeping my shoes clean and shining is very important to me.

That simple lesson often stirs up a fond memory of Daddy Wade. And now, whenever I sit down to clean and polish my shoes, it is a special time with a special meaning.

Thanks, Daddy Wade.

Jim Folks is president of Positive Momentum, a company focused on improving organizational performance. He is a motivational speaker, learning facilitator and executive coach. Folksspeak@aol.com.

110

My Grandfather's Pride

by David Yoho

My mother's father, Felice (Felix) Mignone, was born in Morre de Sanctis, Italy; a town located about 60 kilometers from Naples (Napoli) and located in the mountains of that area. At the age of 20, he and my grandmother, Sylvia, were married. They joined hands and hearts and then, as one, immigrated to the United States. Like so many others, they were in search of a new and better life.

My grandparents were tailors by profession and hard workers by habit. They made a life in America and set about raising their family in one of Philadelphia's working-class neighborhoods. It wasn't always easy; they were of modest means. However, they willingly shared what they had, and they placed high value on proper clothing and overall neatness.

My mom, dad, and I once lived with my grandparents for about a year. It was an interesting time of learning for me. Early one morning, my grandfather stepped out of his bedroom and headed for the bathroom; not an unusual event. He was as properly attired as he could be in the robe he always wore.

Once out in the hallway connecting bedroom to bathroom, my grandfather quickly observed that both my dad and I were already out there. He did an immediate about face; reentering his bedroom. In a few seconds he came out again, but this time he was wearing a *hat*! He had put on his hat because he felt that it was inappropriate to be seen by anyone with uncombed hair.

The man walked his talk of neatness.

David Yoho lives in Louisville, Kentucky., He offers professional education to executives, managers, salespeople and business owners through his speeches, seminars, consultation and educational products.

111

Part-time Grandpa

by George M. Roth

I can recall the many times, as a young boy, I had to listen to my friends boast about their grandparents. I was especially in awe of those friends who had two sets of each—*four* grandparents. The kids would brag about how they were allowed to eat two desserts after dinner, and how they could stay up late whenever they spent the night at Grandma's or Grandpa's house.

At Christmastime, my envy of them would grow even more. I saw how their grandparents always tried to out-give Santa Claus. It was an experience I would have wanted to share.

I was blessed with only one grandmother. She lived far away from us, and I only saw her during summer vacations. I didn't have a grandfather; all my other grandparents had died before I was born.

I was 30 years old before I came to know the true meaning of a grandfather's friendship and had the opportunity to receive the wisdom that perhaps only a grandfather can impart. Let me tell you about it.

The activity director at the local nursing home, a petite, smiling nun, first introduced me to Nick. Nick had moved into this particular facility at the ripe old age of 82. He was, at that time, quite frail; he could no longer get around by himself. Nick needed help.

He had been married in his younger years, but, sadly, his wife died early in the marriage (before they ever had children). Alone and brokenhearted, Nick never remarried. Instead, he focused all his energy on building his business, a very successful electronics company.

Nick was wealthy, but frugal by nature, so very few folks had any idea of his strong financial position. He also enjoyed playing the violin, and took immense satisfaction from his ability to entertain the other residents with his music.

I got to know him. Over the years, our relationship deepened to one of relaxed and close companionship. On occasion, one of his nursing home neighbors would say something like, "So, Nick, this must be your grandson?"

Nick would smile broadly and always respond, "Just part-time ... just part-time."

He was amazing; a philosophical, lighthearted man who combined the great wisdom of his years with an unwavering wit and a genuine kindness. Nick could really shine the light of laughter. He could transform a dreary day into one of sunshine.

One afternoon, as I was signing into the nursing home for a visit with Nick, I was informed that he had suffered a stroke. With deep concern, I hurried along the hallway quietly uttering a simple, but troubled, prayer. I paused at his door, not knowing what to expect. I took a deep breath, opened the door, and entered.

There he was, hooked up to a tangle of wires and IV tubes. He looked frail and pale, but was sitting up in bed. He was actually *smiling*.

As a result of the stroke, experienced at the age of 88, Nick could no longer see; he was virtually blind. I wanted to console him, but I didn't know exactly what to say. I commented, "You must be very angry with God, Nick, for allowing this to happen to you."

He was *not* angry. Nick smiled his special smile and reached for my hand. "George," he said, "I guess I could waste my time and curse God for what happened, for having lost 90 percent of my vision. Perhaps folks would even understand it better if I did." He paused, then continued, "However, I choose to thank Him for the 10 percent of vision I have left because I can still see shadows. Other folks here have had strokes ... and they can't see *at all*."

Initially, I had volunteered at the nursing home to help the elderly, to be of some service, to let those who were without families know that they were not forgotten. I had intended to give something of myself in the process. Instead of giving to Nick, I had received. I was the recipient of a truly precious gift. It came to me in the form of the unselfish compassion demonstrated vividly by an old man with a very young heart.

Although prosperous beyond most people's dreams, Nick did not waste any time counting dollars. Instead, he counted blessings. The yardstick he used to measure life was marked in humility and gratitude.

For more than 10 years, Nick shared with me the value of his experience in life. Much of what I am, and whatever success I have achieved, is due to his encouragement and counsel. As a youngster, I had felt cheated and short-changed in the grandparent department—especially at Christmas. It was only after Nick passed away (at the age of 92) that I fully recognized all the wonderful gifts he had given to me. He showed me how to display faith in the face of adversity. Every day he demonstrated his conviction that, however dire our circumstances, we are still called upon to persevere.

These life-lessons were his precious gifts to me. It was through his persistence and personal enthusiasm that I learned that each of us can stand as a beacon of hope to those with little apparent cause to be grateful.

Nick was my friend, my mentor—my hero. True, we didn't share any genes, and, true, we were just "part-time." But, in all that really counts, he was not only a grandfather, he was *my* grandfather. And I miss him.

George Roth is an award-winning inspirational speaker and author. His imaginative and dynamic keynote presentations generate gratitude for the simple blessings of daily living. (877) 724-7175. George Roth@cardiospecifics.com

112

He Held His Breath

by Norman K. Rebin

Whenever I do die, I expect to "go" just like Grandpa Deda, Efim Alexeievich Rebin, went. When our Russian "Deda" passed away, a part of the four of us who held him in his last moments (Mom, Dad, Sister Lee, and me) died also.

As Deda's grandson and fellow dreamer, I believed him incapable of dying. How could he die? Every ounce of his energies had always been devoted to living. There was an absolute absurdity to any concept connecting Deda and death.

Having lived with him through my high school years, I knew that he was too busy living to ever reflect on dying. Always the adventurer, Deda's eyes would light up while climbing another hill, scaling down another tree, rafting a creek, or just eyeballing one of our bulls on the farm.

He was dedicated to the ideal of unqualified living. Once in the searing prairie heat on our stubble farm, he and I devoured, in one sitting, a gigantic watermelon. With the juice running down his chin, he would spit the seeds and mash the melon's pulp with his even, white teeth; in every way he appeared immensely alive and indestructible. He told me then, as I sat enraptured by his energy, that, if you never stopped living life to its fullest, then you couldn't take time out to die.

So, when Deda stopped breathing in that hospital bed there at St. Paul's in Saskatoon, his last lingering look at us with his deep blue eyes suggested that he'd seen something of such beauty that he was compelled to hold his breath—forever.

I had only seen him hold his breath like that twice before.

The first time was when I was a 10-year-old farm kid. Dad and Deda Efim brought home a Shetland pony (a very small horse, which Deda said was a cross between a tall horse and a short horse). He reasoned that the pony would be perfect for my purposes because I, too, was a cross—a cross between a small man and a big boy. (Deda, an exile to Canada, had been trained to ride bareback by the Cossacks in Russia and was a superb horseman.) As my dad held the reins, I climbed aboard "Beauty" for my very first ride. It was then that Deda held his breath, his face radiant with expectation. So keen was his empathy for my new adventure that I, too, became transformed by his excitement. To this day, almost a half century later, I still see that scene clearly in my mind's eye. And even today, my heartbeat quickens at the memory.

Deda had created a mood of anticipation in me that has lasted my lifetime.

Some years later Deda held his breath a second time. In so doing he made my love affair with Delva sing with his sense of wonder.

During my third year at the University of Saskatchewan, I'd become transfixed by the charm of an 11th-generation American, a physics major. Her brilliant eyes were matched only by her shining intellect. Her color, figure, and personality combined to bewitch and befuddle me. I was smitten beyond redemption.

I asked Delva to come to Blaine Lake to meet Deda and the Rebin clan. The occasion was a triple-sax-featured dance at my hometown's community memorial hall. Deda and all my family and friends would be there. When we arrived he was there, flirting with all the beautiful women (*all* women were beautiful to Deda) and gallantly applauding both the deft dancing steps and dreamy melodies. He left for home in the wee hours of the morning—before we did. He wanted to prepare for our arrival because we were going to spend the night with him.

The dance continued.

We realized, with some concern, that it was now getting close to 4 o'clock in the morning! Deda, even with all his resilience, was now in his 80s and would certainly have gone to bed. As we made our way to his place, through a raging winter blizzard, we felt a bit embarrassed at our temporary thoughtlessness.

Yet, when the door opened to our knock, there he was, still wide-awake, alert, and admiring. As he enveloped us with his eyes and loving arms, I felt his breath catch at the wonder of our love. Even now, after almost 40 years of marriage, Delva and I still feel those arms of his embracing us in his affirmation of our love and our lives.

So, as I watched Deda catch his final breath at St. Paul's Hospital, I knew without a doubt that this was not the end for him; it was but a new and wondrous beginning. Deda had glimpsed the beginning of another great adventure, an adventure so compelling that it would enable him to hold his breath— forever.

Norman Nicalai Rebin (Norm) comes from a long tradition of Norsemen and Russian poets, storytellers, speakers, and adventurers.

113

Special Times in the Wee, Small Hours of the Morning

by Paul Radde

My grandmother used to get up and have her breakfast before anyone else was stirring in the morning; it was usually pitch dark and the house was still. I suppose this was her way of having a little private time to herself as she raised her eight children. At some point, about age 4, I began joining her for breakfast on a regular basis. She would wake me, and we would go downstairs to the kitchen together.

Grandma would fix herself a steaming cup of Postum, then we usually had her favorite breakfast—a piping-hot bowl of Cream of Wheat. She floated a melting pad of butter in the middle, drizzled in some brown sugar, and cooled it off with milk. It was just right.

This was our special time, our time alone without interruption. We would have our little chats every morning. I don't recall our topics, but I know I had lots of questions about her past and how things had been when she was a girl. Other times we would just sit there in the quiet and enjoy being together. It was always calm and serene, a sort of sanctuary.

I felt special. She was the person that older relatives consulted and confided in. During those times, I had the complete and undivided attention of this wise, kind, and loving person; the person everyone else in the family revered and admired. This was a golden hour, one that we continued until I started school; one we shared until my grandmother went to the hospital with a heart attack.

I carried a lot of confidence into life because of my special relationship with my grandmother. It was a confidence no one has shaken, an assurance that began and grew in me because I had this special, separate, private, and personal time every morning with this patient, loving, and caring woman. What a gift she gave me: her presence, her time, and her special attention.

Today I draw validation from those ˙wee hours when my grandmother sought out my company and let me know I was special to her. No one in our entire family had the relationship I had with Grandma. The time we spent together, one-on-one, is her lasting legacy to me.

Dr. Paul Radde is a keynoter who coaches individuals who want to thrive, and organizations that want to achieve a peak performance environment. Explore Thrival, an exceptional state of well-being, through Thrival Systems™. (800) 966-8333. www.Thrival.com

114

Gambling Grandmother

by Timothy G. Burns

My grandmother had a profound impact on my life. I remember her as attentive and loving; someone who always had time to listen and advise. I was sometimes a driven student, and, when struggling with lessons, I was pretty anxious. She never lost patience with me; I needed someone like her. I called her Momie, and she was my rock of stability in a sometimes tumultuous household. No matter what was going on, I could always count on her and turn to her in any time of need.

Momie was of Italian extraction and grew up in New Orleans. Her family owned a grocery store. Well, it was a grocery on the *first* floor; upstairs it was a bookmaking operation where neighbors bet on the horses. Momie said that, when she was young, small bookmaking operations were common in New Orleans—if not quite legal. They were often raided by the authorities. She had lots of stories, such as the occasion when she hid a racing form in a pickle barrel during a raid, then sat on the lid.

Momie came to live with us after my grandfather died. I was quite young. She would often talk about my grandfather and tell of his accomplishments. She was proud of him, and she made me proud of him too. He was a self-made, self-educated man who rose to the rank of colonel in the Army during World War II. After the war he started an engineering and consulting firm in Japan. Tragically, he died there of an illness. I never really knew my grandfather, but I always felt that he was watching me and was always aware of my accomplishments.

Momie liked to gamble. My mother would take her out several times a week to the homes of various women where they played cards. I always envisioned social events, but I later learned that they were really high stakes, smoke-filled poker games.

For her 86th birthday the family took her to Las Vegas for some *serious* gambling. I arrived late, so she gave me my first tour of a Las Vegas casino. Her eyes blazed with excitement as she stood among the swirl of lights and sounds. "Isn't this just wonderful?" she exclaimed.

Later in life she moved to Las Vegas with my aunt and uncle. I tried my best to visit her at least twice a year. Momie loved to introduce me to the dealers, all of whom knew her. She dressed immaculately and wore attractive jewelry (and she *didn't* care to discuss her age). Once, when she was losing, I loaned her $20.00 and her luck apparently changed. She later told me, "Tim, I won back all the money I lost except *your* $20.00."

She would still visit us on holidays. We always had a great time. On Christmas day in 1995, however, she fell and broke her hip. She was 95. She was with our family when it happened, but no one was able to catch her or break her fall.

I followed the ambulance to the hospital, hoping for the best, fearing the worst. While she was in the emergency room, I offered prayer in the hospital chapel. With tear-filled eyes, I stared at the crucifix of the One whose birthday we had been celebrating.

"Why Momie?" I asked. To my complete astonishment I received a response: the assurance that she would recover.

She went into surgery the next day. The operation was a success. The doctor was not sure, however, if she would ever walk again. With Momie drifting in and out of consciousness, the next few days were difficult indeed. I placed angels around the room and played soothing music.

By New Year's Day, Momie was showing improvement (enough that she made a few bets on the bowl games). Full recovery was still a long way off, but she was telling everyone, including the hospital personnel, that she would be going back to Vegas. She was the only one not surprised when, 30 days later, she boarded a plane for Nevada, with only the aid of a walker.

While her doctors were truly astonished at her speedy recovery, I knew the true reason. Momie was highly motivated.

She wanted to get back home to the blackjack tables.

Tim Burns, CPA, is a practicing accountant and professional speaker in the areas of entrepreneurship, taxes, and estate planning. (505) 838-0019. TGBurns@aol.com

Afterword

As a publisher, I knew *GRAND-Stories* was a winner from my first glance at the manuscript. As a son, grandson, father and brand-new grandfather, I was touched by these stories. I was especially pleased to see them come together in this book. We at Friendly Oaks Publications hope you have enjoyed them.

Unless you've ever put together a book from raw ideas into something you can see, touch and hold in your hands, it's difficult to imagine the amount of work that's involved. But I had a dedicated partner in this project—the author, Ernie Wendell. It was a true partnership in every sense of the word. I'll genuinely miss the calls, the faxes and the endless stream of e-mails we shared almost daily.

With this book, Ernie adds an exciting, new program to his keynote presentations. If you like this book, you'll love his portrayal as "Grandpa Ernie" in person. Here's how to contact him:

Ernie Wendell
Grandparents Universal
1308 Kent Street
Durham, NC 27707
(877) 595-6000 (toll free)

We're already collecting stories for *GRAND-Stories II*. We'd love to hear from you. Send your grandparent stories to Ernie at the above address, or to me at **Friendly Oaks Publications, P.O. Box 672, Pleasanton, TX 78064**. If we print your story, we'll acknowledge you as the author and will send you a copy of the finished book with our compliments.

—James D. Sutton
Friendly Oaks Publications
Pleasanton, Texas

We have included this order form for those who would like to make *GRAND-Stories* available to friends and relatives.

Order Form

Price: $21.95

Sales tax: Add 8.25% if shipped to Texas address

Shipping & handling: $4.00

Payment method: (check one)

_____Check _____Visa _____MasterCard

Card #:_____

Expiration date:_____

Name on card:_____

Signature:_____

Address postal orders to:

Friendly Oaks Publications
P.O. Box 662
Pleasanton, TX 78064

Phone orders: Call (830) 569-3586 or Fax: (830) 281-2617
Ship books to:

Name:_____

Address:_____

City/State/Zip:_____

Phone:_____

Use the space below to write the grandest *GRAND-Story* (YOURS!)

_____

_____

_____

_____

_____

_____

_____

_____

_____

_____

_____

_____

_____

_____

_____

_____

_____

_____

_____

_____

_____

Use the space below to write the grandest *GRAND-Story* (YOURS!)

_____

_____

_____

_____

_____

_____

_____

_____

_____

_____

_____

_____

_____

_____

_____

_____

_____

_____

_____

_____

Use the space below to write the grandest *GRAND-Story* (YOURS!)

_____

_____

_____

_____

_____

_____

_____

_____

_____

_____

_____

_____

_____

_____

_____

_____

_____

_____

_____

_____

Use the space below to write the grandest *GRAND-Story* (YOURS!)

_____

_____

_____

_____

_____

_____

_____

_____

_____

_____

_____

_____

_____

_____

_____

_____

_____

_____

_____

Use the space below to write the grandest *GRAND-Story* (YOURS!)

_____

_____

_____

_____

_____

_____

_____

_____

_____

_____

_____

_____

_____

_____

_____

_____

_____

_____

_____

_____

Use the space below to write the grandest *GRAND-Story* (YOURS!)

_____

_____

_____

_____

_____

_____

_____

_____

_____

_____

_____

_____

_____

_____

_____

_____

_____

_____

_____

Use the space below to write the grandest *GRAND-Story* (YOURS!)

_____

_____

_____

_____

_____

_____

_____

_____

_____

_____

_____

_____

_____

_____

_____

_____

_____

_____

Use the space below to write the grandest *GRAND-Story* (YOURS!)

_____

_____

_____

_____

_____

_____

_____

_____

_____

_____

_____

_____

_____

_____

_____

_____

_____

_____

Use the space below to write the grandest *GRAND-Story* (YOURS!)

_____

_____

_____

_____

_____

_____

_____

_____

_____

_____

_____

_____

_____

_____

_____

_____

_____

_____

Use the space below to write the grandest *GRAND-Story* (YOURS!)

Use the space below to write the grandest *GRAND-Story* (YOURS!)

_____

_____

_____

_____

_____

_____

_____

_____

_____

_____

_____

_____

_____

_____

_____

_____

_____

_____

_____

_____

Use the space below to write the grandest *GRAND-Story* (YOURS!)